# From
# Istanbul
## to
# Aghtamar

An Armenian Pilgrimage

# From
# Istanbul
## to
# Aghtamar

## By Hagop Nersoyan

Ashod Press, New York, 1990

FIRST EDITION


Library of Congress Cataloging-in-Publication Data

Nersoyan, H. J. (Hagop J.)
    From Istanbul to Aghtamar : an Armenian pilgrimage / by Hagop    Nersoyan.
        p.    cm.
    ISBN   0-935102-27-2  :  $10.00
    1. Armenian Church—Turkey—History—20th century.   2. Tur-
key—Description and travel—1981-   3. Nersoyan, H. J. (Hagop J.)
—Journeys—Turkey.   4. Surb Khach' Ekeghets' i (Van †li. Turkey)   5. Turkey—Church history.   6. Oriental Orthodox churches
—Turkey —History—20th century.     I.  Title.
BX124. T8N47      1990                                          90-45117
281 ' . 62 ' 09561—dc20                                        CIP

## Acknowledgment

I thank Marie Mesrobian Nersoyan for remedying the lapses of my memory during the writing of the text. I also thank Florence Avakian, Nona Balakian, Dr. Avedis Sanjian, and particularly the Rev. Arten Ashjian for reading the manuscript, for their encouragement, and for corrections they were able to suggest.

In Memory of
His Beatitude
Archbishop Shnork Kalousdian
Armenian Patriarch of Turkey
1913 — 1990

*This is a SHAN book.*

# From
# Istanbul
## to
# Aghtamar

Archbishop Shnork Kalousdian, Patriarch of the Armenians of Turkey, died in the night of March 6-7, 1990.

We were good friends. He had once written to me of the "reciprocity of our feeling." We are friends of long years, he had said, "and you have never left my memory. You often visit the house of my memory in a very special way, even at times when I do not have to write to you."

Our friendship began to develop around 1950 when he was still a vardapet, the priest of the Armenian parishes of Paterson and Newark, New Jersey. I remember the time when he gave me the key to his black Dodge. "I won't need it for a couple of days," he had said. When I returned it to his Paterson home the next day at noon, I was hungry, and "raided" his refrigerator. In it were two eggs, a bottle of milk, half full, a piece of cheese, perhaps a bunch of radishes and a loaf of bread. "That's my lunch. We'll share it," he said. He also remembered that there was a bottle of beer somewhere if I didn't mind its not being chilled. Did he have any butter? I would volunteer to scramble the eggs. "If you can't eat them raw, you'll have to boil yours," he said.

Particularly in his younger days, and in certain moods Archbishop Shnork had a way of murmuring to himself: *Hoy Nazan im, Nazan im* . . . He had a story explaining the habit. It is told again in a biographical sketch of him researched and written by Robert Haddecyan, and published on the twenty-fifth anniversary of his enthronement. The story goes back to the time when he was a boy of ten at an orphanage in Lebanon where there was, as he vividly remembered, an American missionary woman who preached every Sunday "in Armenian, imagine!" He remembered also becoming seriously ill one day, with a contagious disease. In the room next to his was a little girl equally sick. A few days later Arshag (the future Archbishop Shnork) was surprised to hear the girl sing an Armenian song in a voice that seemed to be coming from beyond the grave: *Hoy Nazan im, Nazan im, Nazan tou parov yegar* . . . The girl died that same afternoon. They told Arshag in his sickbed that during the funeral service swallows had flown into the chapel through a window, circled the bare wooden coffin, and flown back out. *Hoy Nazan im, Nazan im.* Archbishop Shnork never forgot that voice. In it he kept hearing the sadness of the circumstances that brought them all to that orphanage.

He once mentioned his practice of keeping a record of his experiences each day. One entry in his diary is about his forty-day retreat immediately after his ordination to the priesthood at the Armenian Monastery of Saint James in Jerusalem. All Armenian priests are required canonically to go through that retreat, which is also a period of intensive apprenticeship, when the newly-ordained priest learns the art of celebrating the Mass or Divine Liturgy (*badarak* in Armenian, the equivalent of the Latin *oblatio*). The retreat is reminiscent of the 40 days that Jesus spent in the wilderness prior to his ministry. The original intent of the retreat was to prepare, through prayer and abstinence, for the awesome responsibility of being God's instrument in leading people to their eternal salvation, for the uncommon privilege of performing the rite wherewith bread and wine would change into the blood and body of Christ. Ordination is itself in a sense a new baptism. The ordaining bishop gives the ordinand a new name to indicate that he, the bishop, is the ordinand's spiritual parent, and that the ordinand is a new man in a new dispensation, now qualified to perform specific duties in the house of the Lord.

Arshag went into the priesthood with the full awareness of the requirements of his calling. He was ordained with a companion who eventually left the priesthood. They were a few days into the retreat when a feeling that approached anxiety seized Father Shnork: What he hoped would happen was not happening. The circumstances surrounding the retreat were far from ideal, and what made matters even worse was that his companion did not care.

There they were, at the chapel of Saint Thoros, for supposedly secluded, quiet meditation. But close to the chapel were dwellings inhabited by chattering elderly, loud teenagers, and squalling infants—families that had fled persecution and famine, and found refuge in the Monastery. He had nevertheless wanted the retreat to be, not a mere formality but a genuine experience, a receiving of strength from God for his life ahead, a time of contemplation in an appropriate environment. But he learned to endure the disturbing intrusions with patient understanding. At the same time he despaired that the circumstances that troubled him seemed symptomatic of the condition of the Armenian Church in general.

In his diary of 1935 he records his feelings on the day before his first *badarak*. He is 22: "Today, having come out of our cell at Saint Thoros, we were led to [the Monastery of] Saint James. There, after kissing the hand of the Patriarch, of holy lineage, we stood before the altar. When the time came to recite the prayer 'Merciful Father,' I drew near with emotion and trembling of heart, kissed the cross and hand of the Patriarch, and said my prayer. My voice was very weak. I could not muster the proper spiritual disposition that must accompany a prayer. Thus my first prayer seemed to me to be a failure, both as the performance of a formality and as a properly intoned elocution, but most of all as prayer. With an unhappy disposition I left the church and was led back to Saint Thoros. That same evening I read in a book entitled *Sermons* . . . the sermon about the Good Thief . . . It was truly an admirable sermon. I had decided to read the whole book that evening. Darkness set in, and [my companion and] I retired."

To qualify for the rank or degree of vardapet the future

Patriarch wrote a thesis on St. Paul's First Epistle to the Corinthians where the Apostle expatiates on the themes of Christian purity, holiness, devotion to the Lord. Father Shnork kept his interest in these subjects throughout his life. As a student, he was most interested in history and geography, as well as canon law. But sanctity is the dominant topic of his extensive writings.

Archbishop Shnork was saintly, even if not a saint in the traditional, somewhat arcane meaning of the word. It is not likely that the blind will see and the lame walk by invoking his name. He did make occasional concessions to interests that could be said to be worldly. "I should go to Florida so my bones will warm up a bit," he would say. He might have been a bit more farsighted where the issue was the Patriarchate's money which was under his control. The fact remains that he let no inclination interfere seriously with his principal aim in life: Steady progress toward the achievement of holiness.

Two scenes compete in the image I cherish of Archbishop Shnork. The first I can only imagine: The painful circumstances of his farewell to the world. This true prince of the church who, by the inscrutable will of the God whom he so selflessly served, fell down the marble stairs of the residence of the Catholicos of All Armenians, cracked his skull, and died an agonizing death—with a Psalm on his lips. Though revelatory of the man, this will not be my dominant recollection of Archbishop Shnork. I will remember him rather as I beheld him on that June morning of 1989, atop Mount Nemrut, in Anatolia, at an altitude of over 7,000 feet.

Mount Nemrut is renowned for the colossal statues, among them Ahura Mazda (Aramazt, to the Armenians), that adorn its peak. They were commissioned and placed at the east terrace of the peak by King Antiochus I of Commagene, now roughly the province of Adiyaman in Turkey. Antiochus I lived in the first century BC, a contemporary of the Armenian emperor Tigran the Great. Nemrut was not the highest among the hills that surrounded it. That did not please Antiochus, surnamed *Soter* (savior), who wanted to be buried there. He corrected the deficiency by making his slaves carry up rocks to increase the height of the hill by another 150 feet.

A number of pilgrims, Marie and I among them, were there at the top of the small mountain with the Patriarch, on our way back from Aghtamar. We had been awakened that morning at our hotel in the village of Kahta at about two o'clock, for the long, bumpy ride in an old vehicle to a car port at some distance from our destination, where we were glad to find a refreshment and souvenir stand. The hot tea we were served in small glasses was most welcome, for the air felt thinner already, and some of us were sorry we were not wearing warmer clothing. Why hadn't somebody told us? From here we continued our ascent on foot.

The pebbly road up to Mount Nemrut is hazardous, almost demanding the surefootedness of a goat. When we reached the summit the Patriarch was already there, wrapped in a blanket, a brimless hat with straight sides and a flat crown covering his head.

The high altitude, the closeness of the sky, the huge torsos of the gods with their heads sitting before them on the ground gave the place an extramundane character. As the light gradually increased, the hills around us seemed to emerge from a primeval dark. In this extraordinary place it was as if we, who had been together for days, had not seen each other for a long time.

An icy, strong wind seemed to be blowing from all sides all at once and, unless you had had the foresight of being properly protected, it shook your whole body. The Patriarch who never liked cold weather did not look comfortable even with his blanket. "Where are the taller men? Stand around him! Closer! Don't let the wind get to him!" someone ordered. And so they did. The deacons and choir members, all of us pilgrims stood facing east. We were about to see what the gods themselves were placed there to see morning after morning. The sunrise. "It is spectacular, worth the effort," the Patriarch had said to me.

As the first millimeter of the emerging fiery ball appeared the Patriarch, surrounded by those who took the cold to shield him from it, began to sing *Aravod Lousso* in his characteristic voice. Not, as singing voices go, a pleasant one, but rather an unsettling voice that seemed to come from cavernous depths.

That is how I will remember Patriarch Shnork: Standing erect to greet the rising star of day, with a broken Aramazt behind him, singing with all his might the most popular Armenian religious song, written by the most grace-filled of Armenian poets. I shall remember his face illumined by the growing light even as he sang that song of Saint Nersess, all thirty-six stanzas of it, each stanza celebrating a letter of the Armenian alphabet, each letter worked into the worship of the God of his Fathers.

There are rare patriarchs who are actualy described, not routinely honored, by the periphrastic designation "his beatitude." Archbishop Shnork was such a patriarch.

His Beatitude had graciously invited my wife and me to join the 1989 pilgrims to the tenth century Holy Cross Church on the Island of Aghtamar (Akdamar on Turkish maps) on Lake Van. When I talked to him on the telephone at his residence in Istanbul to inquire whether we could join another pilgimage "maybe next time," I sensed in his reply a mixture of amusement and vexation. "Next time?" he said. "But there may not *be* a next time. If you want to see our towns and the remnants of our churches and people in the interior of Turkey, I suggest that you be here a few days before our departure. Do not forget, you are my guests," he added.

On our arrival at the Patriarchate Archbishop Shnork greeted us on the second floor. He said my name accenting the first syllable and dwelling on the second (as people do when they see a friend after a long absence) and put his arms around me even as I was bending to kiss his hand. He greeted Marie with equal warmth. Then he proceeded to give us a tour of the building. He made a point of not having us miss the three large priceless Ayvazovskys that are hung around the landing on the way up to his residence. "They are in need of restoration," he said.

Our pilgrimage had begun . . . at the Patriarchate of Istanbul.

I was not surprised to see Archbishop Shnork look rather frail in his dark gray cassock. A beard, now entirely white, draped his ascetic face, covering rather densely the upper part of his chest. The white hair at the back of his bald head was left untrimmed.

Several portraits of him as well as sketches and photographs by a number of artists were on the walls of various rooms in the Patriarchate. As I examined these representations of him with care, I was impressed by the fidelity with which the artists had caught the deep piety, compassion, integrity and moral courage of the Archbishop in the lines of his lean, high cheek bones, his forthright look, the attentive mellowness of his eyes—always almost sad, yet about to break into a smile.

We were his guests at dinner that evening. He knew that one piece of luggage had not arrived with us at the Istanbul airport. That became a personal concern. He instructed his aides to keep calling the airport, and fetch the waylaid luggage as soon as it arrived (which it did three days later). The conversation turned on a subject about which I had written to him earlier: The project, not yet fully publicized, to canonize the victims of the 1915 Massacres, to declare them all saints. I did not think he would be in favor of it, and he was not. I gave him the reasons why I myself happen to be opposed to the project. "Unfortunately the issue has been politicized," he said. "It has become a contest as to who will do the *popular* thing. We do not want to oppose the idea outright, because we do not want to create the false impression that we are indifferent to the tragic fate of those who lost their lives . . . A wise course would be to continue to do what we now do, but officially. We must make it mandatory, through an entry in our church calendar, to remember the victims of the Massacres, preferably on the Sunday after Easter, by holding a service for the repose of their souls." We talked of other matters.

As the dinner concluded, he told us that it is his habit to watch the evening news in the library. Most of the news was about the fate of the Turks in Bulgaria. They are being oppressed, the anchorwoman said. There were scenes of Turks gathering their meager belongings and heading for Turkey. Knowing as we did that the treatment of the Turks was not nearly as brutal as the suffering the Turks themselves had inflicted on the Armenians, a natural tendency was to smile, though the reaction brought neither solace nor satisfaction.

From some comments the Patriarch made, it was clear that he kept abreast of what was going on in his country and around the world. As the last commercials came on, he told us the schedule he had prepared for us for the next day, and he retired. The next day we were invited to lunch by Khachig Mardinian at one of the most renowned seaside restaurants of Istanbul, the Kosova. Each of the three varieties of lamb was more savory than the others.

The Patriarchate of the Armenians of Turkey is located on the European side of Istanbul, in a section of the Old City (Eski Istanbul) called Kumkapi. It is a grand wooden building which was used at one time as offices only. In its reception hall hang the pictures of the more illustrious of the ecclesiastics who occupied the patriarchal throne since its inception in 1461, such luminaries as Golod, Nalian, Khrimian, Varzhabedian, Ormanian, Tourian, and the immediate predecessor of Kalousdian, Karekin Khachadourian.

Any Armenian in Istanbul over 35 years of age remembers Patriarch Karekin Khachadourian (Drabizoni), a close friend of Patriarch Shnork. I myself never met him but recall his name with a feeling of closeness, for I used his textbook, *The Light of the World Among the Armenians*, when I was a church school teacher in my mid teens in Aleppo, Syria. In the life of Archbishop Karekin one can see reflected the change in the condition of the Armenian people in Asia Minor from the last quarter of the nineteenth century to the middle of the twentieth.

The nineteenth century is the laboratory where the chemistry of the Armenian psyche changed in a radical way. Before that period we recognized ourselves as a *religious* community; by the time the century drew to a close our self-recognition was in *national* terms.

The new anti-religious, anti-clerical, atheistic consciousness needed a symbol, something to give it focus. It was found—"the nation." The nation—anyone's, whether Armenian, Greek, Pole, Palestinian, Jew, Turk or other—is an ideal because there does not seem to be anything supernatural, hence questionable, about it. "The nation" is, moreover, a most flexible notion, a Procrustean concept. It can be a terminal for any train of collective passion. We all need something to dedicate ourselves to, something bigger than ourselves. The nation may not be big enough to serve the whole world, but that is precisely how we want it. It is big enough to serve *us*. No one knows when the nation begins, and we can assume that it will be there forever. No one knows its limits. So it is, you see, infinite. It is a beautiful god, the perfect god to replace the other, old-wives'-tale one, the one that begins with a capital G. And if one surrenders oneself to it with sufficient passion, it may even promise immortality!

Archbishop Karekin, an alert, conscientious, highly educated clergyman, sought to guard the people against the excesses of this novel orientation toward secularism, this (often covert) denial of our roots in universal Christianity. His biography is important because it reflects the history of the Armenian community in Turkey before and after 1915. Patriarch Karekin could do things that Patriarch Shnork could not, because the freedoms of the Armenian community in Turkey, meager to begin with, continued to dwindle.

Trabzon is the ancient Greek colonial city of Trapezus, on the southeastern angle of the Black sea. Archbishop Karekin was born there in 1880, and was baptized as Khachig. It is the city two of whose better known mosques, Ortahisar and Yenijuma, were formerly the Greek churches of the Virgin of the Golden Head and of Saint Eugenius. In the sixth century Trabzon was the chief city of the Northern Province of Greater Armenia on the map of Mauricius Flavius Tiberius, the Armenian emperor of Byzantium, whom our historians refer to simply as Morig. In 1880 the Armenian population of Constantinople had reached a peak of 300,000, while Trabzon was one of the 44 dioceses under the jurisdiction of the patriarch.

Khachig was 14 when an Armenian "provocation" (as the Turks called it, contrary to the findings of a careful investigation conducted by the British) became a pretext for a massacre in Sassoun. The carnage was carried out mostly by the Kurds who wanted all to themselves the fertile lands and the grass-rich hills of the region. The Armenians had succeeded in repulsing a first attack, but the Kurds were able to return because the Turkish military command formed a whole division composed exclusively of Kurds. Organized under the name of Hamidiye, they were to be used opposite the Cossacks in the interminable wars between the Ottoman and Russian empires. After their initial defeat, and now supported by the regular Ottoman army, the Kurds of Sassoun did succeed the second time: By nightfall on August 28, 10,000 Armenians had been murdered.

In 1895 Sultan Abdulhamid again reacted in his characteristic way to Armenian requests that elementary human rights be respected in the empire. This time the atrocities began on September 26, in Khachig's home city of Trabzon. From there they radiated with deadly accuracy to every city and village of Anatolia. It was as if a demon were guiding the lava of an eruption of human bestiality along paths marked by the presence of Armenians. They were killed by the sword, or drowned or hanged. Shops and homes were looted. Churches were ransacked, holy images desecrated, vessels put to obscene use. Husbands and wives, parents and children, siblings and relatives were slaughtered before each other's eyes. Women were publicly raped, little girls violated. Men were tortured, mutilated, then left to die in spreading puddles of their blood. Priests and monks were specific targets of forced conversion to Islam. Monasteries were devastated. It was particularly frightful in some cities, Van among them. In Diyarbakir and elsewhere Armenian churches were packed with people, then burned with the doors bolted from the outside. The indiscriminate butchery of 300,000 victims lasted three months.

A year after these massacres Khachig left Trabzon to study in Istanbul. He went on from there to the Mourad Raphaelian (Armenian Roman Catholic) school in Venice. He returned to Istanbul and enrolled in the reorganized Armenian Seminary of Armash, where he was ordained a celibate priest.

In addition to parish priests, the churches of Istanbul had then each its own *karozich* or preacher who would have to be a vardapet in the literal meaning of the word, namely an (authorized) teacher (of orthodox doctrine). Traditionally the better known parishes had the more erudite of the preachers. Father Karekin served in various churches in that capacity, then became the dean of the Armenian Seminary of Sis. He returned to Istanbul in 1909, to undertake the editorship of *Dajar* (Cathedral). He was 29.

It has been estimated that some two hundred Armenian periodicals were published in Istanbul between 1850 and 1914. These included two in Turkish: *Cerideyi Sarkiye* and *Manzumeyi*

*Efkiar*. Many brilliant Armenian literary and scholarly careers began in one or the other of these publications. Istanbul was then one of the three most vibrant centers of Armenian culture (Venice and Tbilisi the other two). The best of French, Italian or German fiction or poetry found its echoes in Armenian Istanbul, which thus was not without its own influence on the Turkish intelligentsia. The theater, including the comedy of manners, flourished. At the same time dedicated, talented individuals were in search of Armenian authenticity, engaging in what may be called a cultural archaeology. Grammatical rules were established for a modern Armenian that had almost entirely replaced the classical. Truly Armenian music and folklore were unearthed and revived. All the differences of opinions, rivalries and hostilities were there, signifying a rare period of popular and cultural vitality.

When Karekin Vardapet returned to Istanbul, a constitutional regime was, or at least seemed to be, in effect in the capital. On July 24, 1908, Abdulhamid had restored the constitution that he had proclaimed once before—then dismissed—in December, 1876. It was generally felt that subsequent to the bloodless revolution of the Young Turks the Sultan would have to abide by the terms of the document that diluted his power and made liberty, fraternity, equality and justice possible. What a previous generation of discontented citizens, led by liberal men like Namik Kemal Bey and Zia Pasha, had called "Ottomanism" was about to be realized: all the religious and ethnic elements of the empire would coexist, each in pursuit of its collective artistic, intellectual and spiritual ends, under the same banner!

A number of Armenian writers who had left Turkey in despair returned to the country they still loved. They had been led to think that racial differences were no longer to prevent the rebuilding, shoulder to shoulder with all other enlightened citizens, of the new empire, the free commonwealth of the future. Leading Armenians returned to Turkey as an unnaturally abused child is wont to return, lured by the attraction of home, on the promise that he will not be bloodied again. There were of course in Turkey itself virulent rivalries between the conservative adherents of the old order and the reform-minded extremists, but the resolution of the conflict in favor of modern ways was, so the progressive elements thought, only a matter of time.

Among those who returned was Vahan Tekeyan, the greatest of the Western Armenian poets of this century.

Nothing in Armenian literature captures with greater economy the stunning, dreadful transition from the euphoria of 1908 to the nightmare of 1915 than a poem of Tekeyan, entitled *Something Terrible There*. In just 21 lines Tekeyan portrays the Monstrosity that wrapped itself around the feet, gnawed at the chest, reached the neck, the eyes, and sank its fangs directly into the brain of a whole nation.

Even as the imprisonment, banishment and execution of leading Armenian intellectuals ominously heralded the Genocide of 1915, Karekin Vardapet was the Primate of Konya, engaged in the construction of a school for boys and girls. The school was left unfinished. In August of that year he had the good fortune of being sent to Jerusalem, as a teacher at the Armenian Seminary.

In the tragic years between 1913 and 1922 the Patriarch of Istanbul was Archbishop Zaven Der Yeghiayan. He was elected in 1913. A year after the beginning of the Genocide, in 1916, Turkish militia escorted him from Istanbul to Baghdad by order of the minister of the Interior. The time was one of utter desperation. Archbishop Zaven did all it was in his power to do. He repeatedly appealed to the Turkish authorities to put an end to the wholesale carnage. Two years after his banishment he found himself in Mosul. Then the British occupied that city and the Patriarch was free. He traveled to Port Said in 1919, where he received an exuberant welcome by the Armenians of Egypt. That same year, while massacres and rumors of massacres were still of great concern, he returned to his see in Istanbul on a British battleship. One remarkable thing about Archbishop Zaven is that between 1913 and 1922 he ordained close to 30 priests. One would think he was hearkening to the Psalmist: "The sorrows of death compassed me, and the pains of hell gat hold upon me: I found trouble and sorrow. Then called I upon the name of the Lord." Shortly after his return to Istanbul Patriarch Zaven called Karekin Vardapet to Turkey and sent him to Trabzon, for that diocese had been left without a Primate. As locum tenens the young vardapet tried to reclaim the Armenian church properties and educate the orphans. His petitions were not ignored then, but there is no Armenian presence in Trabzon today.

Karekin Vardapet was consecrated bishop in Etchmiadzin in 1922, and returned to Istanbul in 1923. That was the year when Mustafa Kemal Pasha had the destiny of Turkey entirely in his hands, and was trying to rescue it from anarchy. The leaders of the Young Turks who had ordered the Armenian genocide had fled to Germany, and Mohammed VI, the last sultan (who was willing to have European Powers take over and rule his land) had been exiled. From 1922 (the year of the Sultan's exile) to 1927 the Armenian Patriarchate of Constantinople had no incumbent. Bishop Karekin was proposed as candidate under the new political conditions, but he declined. He traveled to California instead, as the Legate of the Catholicos of All Armenians. From then to 1950, while Primate of the Armenian diocese of Marseille, France, and subsequently Legate of the Catholicos of All Armenians in South America, he edited scholarly periodicals, wrote books of historical and religious interest, and translated the New Testament, as well as the works of Gregory of Narek and Yeznik of Goghp from classical into modern Armenian. When he became Patriarch of the Armenians of Turkey in 1950, some of the pre-genocide vitality of the Armenian community was still discernible. Ninety-nine delegates who formed the Armenian General Assembly cast votes. Fourteen of these were clergymen. There were 85 laymen, 15 of whom were from

the interior of Turkey. (Eleven years later at the election of
Archbishop Shnork as the eighty-second patriarch, the
number of delegates from the interior was reduced to seven.
There were 72 lay delegates from Istanbul, and only ten
clergymen. A married priest was then the locum tenens. The
Turkish government had informed him that it had not as yet
decided on such laws as would constitute a permanent
framework within which the election of the Armenian
patriarch could take place. Thus the delegates who elected
Archbishop Shnork had assembled together on an *ad hoc* basis,
and dispersed after the election.)

Archbishop Karekin's incumbency is marked by two
achievements that were difficult then, and would be more
difficult, if not impossible today. They are both acts of optimism, based on the assumption that the Armenian community of Turkey is, so to speak, reclaimable. They also
indicate of course the state of mind of the community and
of charitable agencies that made the realization of the projects
in question possible.

One evening, on the porch of his summer residence
Patriarch Shnork said to me: "Even as late as 1961, when I
was elected, I was certain that if, due to some unimaginable
turn of events, the Armenian people were to vanish from the
face of the earth, the very last Armenian would be found here,
in Istanbul."

That feeling was of course even stronger in 1950. Not long
after his election Patriarch Karekin managed to establish an
Armenian Seminary in Istanbul. He had relied on the gener-
osity of his people, the Gulbenkian Foundation, and on "our
government which, being broadminded, liberal and of healthy
judgment, has grasped the importance of education." An
Armenian, M. Shellefian, was then a member of the Turkish
parliament. That too helped.

The purpose of the Seminary was, first, to prepare able
and decent human beings; and second, good and virtuous
citizens who would "follow the calling determined for them

by God." Fifty-three students enrolled for the very first academic year of the Seminary in 1954. Today the "Seminary" (*Tbrevank*) is no longer a seminary. It is an ordinary school with a student body of 169.

The second notable achievement of Patriarch Karekin was his role in the building or rebuilding of the Armenian church in Istanbul, at Galatya. Obtaining a permit for the building of anything has always been a hassle for the Armenians of Turkey both during and after Ottoman rule. There were times when the authorities required that the building of a church be completed in no more than 40 days, their way of preventing the church from being a prominent and impressive structure. The church at Galatya was, in August 1965, the very first church in and around Istanbul, built in the traditional Armenian style, with the characteristic polygonal pointed cupola. The permit for its construction had been obtained and the work was under way when Archbishop Karekin died. The days of the consecration of the completed church by Archbishop Shnork remain outstandingly memorable in the annals of Armenian Istanbul.

Little if any is left today of the formidable clout that a patriarch had in the days of the Ottoman Empire. Before World War I the Patriarch of Constantinople had jurisdiction over the Catholicosate of Cilicia, the Catholicosate of Aghtamar (which came to an end in 1895), and the Patriarchate of Jerusalem.

Patriarch Shnork was indifferent to the loss of the secular power enjoyed by his predecessors except as it affected the well-being of his people and deprived them collectively of some basic rights. He was first and foremost a prince of the church, and only secondarily the secular chief of his community. He had no patience with the niceties of theology, which he regarded as a source of discord, and hence a source of factionalism in the otherwise one flock of Christ. "But the averment that the church is one—that in itself is a theological claim," I said to him once in the course of a conversation in the cool of an evening on the porch of his summer residence. "Well, yes," he said, "but you must allow there is a limit beyond which discussants lose sight of the faith and try to outsmart each other." He said it with authority. I did not pursue the matter.

In the performance of his episcopal and administrative duties Patriarch Shnork put the church and its proper objective ahead of every other consideration, but without losing sight of the importance of financial solvency. "He runs the Patriarchate with the same frugality he runs his own life," someone once said to me. The remark was probably not meant to be a compliment.

On the way to and from Van we pilgrims visited various cities — cities that teemed with Armenians as late as the first decade of this century. Many of these Armenians were individuals of culture, or of enterprise and wealth. Each city used to have an Armenian bishop of its own, with at least one cathedral, usually a monastery, and one or more schools under the bishop's jurisdiction.

In the absence of accurate censuses the number of Armenians who lived in Anatolia prior to 1914 cannot be determined with much precision. A large number of records that may have been useful were burned or destroyed. Even where there are official enumerations of citizens only the adult males are counted. Fairly accurate calculations yield nevertheless a total in excess of two million, of whom some 600,000 survived the Massacres of 1915, some by sheer luck, some because of resistance, and others owing to the humanity of individual Turks (officials as well as ordinary citizens) who refused to obey the orders of murder and exile, and took their Armenian friends or neighbors under their protection.

A. N. Mnatsaganian, an Armenian social scientist, in his book, *Tragedy of the Armenian People*, calculates that the total number of Armenians killed between 1882 and 1922 was two million thirty-seven thousand eight hundred and sixty. One way of disparaging Christianity during all the horror was to remove bells from church towers and in their stead hang dogs by their tails. The howls of the dogs replaced the peals of the bells.

As the careers of Patriarchs Zaven and Karekin indicate, at no time did the Armenian Church as a whole surrender to the fear of extinction. It is as if it were exhibiting all along the faith of Saint Gregory, the third/fourth century enlightener of the people. Thrown into a dark dungeon, in the midst of poisonous creeping creatures, the Enlightener was nevertheless confident that he would again see the light of day to resume his interrupted work, the conversion of Armenia. There are presently Armenian men and women in Turkey who insist on being themselves, an attitude that does not in any way involve or imply a threat to any morally sound, reasonable Turkish interest.

The history of the Armenian Patriarchate of historic Constantinople, which begins probably with Hovakim (1461-1478), a protege of Sultan Mehmet II Fatih (the Conqueror), is not consistently pretty. There was a time when men vied for the position and often had recourse to means less than honorable to topple the incumbent patriarch. A common strategy was to make "friends" in important circles, that is, as close to the sultan as possible, then use them toward the fulfillment of wicked designs. In the latter part of the seventeenth century corruption reached the ultimate in depravity: a married priest, named Andreas, who bribed his way to the patriarchal see, was nicknamed *Jehennem Merdiveni* (Staircase to Hell). His successor, also a married priest, was an illiterate peasant. The job of patriarch conferred power and prestige; it could be bought and sold, and the expended amount could be a good investment. The patriarch collected taxes, and had revenues from real estate and other sources. Nearly anyone could get the job who was sufficiently ambitious, knew the right people, was clever enough, and had no moral decency.

Early in the seventeenth century the troubles of the Patriarchate had been compounded by the efforts of Latin, or Armenian Latinizing, clerics—supported notably by France—to have the Armenians of Turkey join the Roman Catholic Church. Latinophile tendencies were instrumental in moving the Patriarchate from Samatia to its present location. The move was completed in 1641.

Beginning with about the first quarter of the eighteenth century—the century of the European *Aufklärung*—the situation changed. The see was then occupied by a number of archbishops, dedicated to ecclesiastical revival and progress, who therefore placed considerable emphasis on Armenian church doctrine and general scholarship. Then the situation underwent a radical change again in the middle of the nineteenth century, as already noted. That change had been in the making for several decades, its effects still very much in evidence among the Armenians around the world: Ideas trickling down from European writers, from the French *philosophes*, Jean-Jacques Rousseau in particular, the French Revolution itself inspiring the people with the heady notions of nationalism and secularism.

In the first half of the nineteenth century individual self-recognition was still largely in terms of the class to which one belonged: There were the *amiras*, the wealthy financiers, merchants and industrialists who, in the absence of a nobility, constituted the highest echelon of Armenian society in Istanbul. Often referred to as "prince," an amira was socially well-connected, although the slightest suspicion of disloyalty to the sultan, or even an accusation to that effect, was enough to have him exiled or decapitated.

Below the amiras were the professional men, lawyers, physicians, educators, who were given the title of *efendi*, a term which eventually became the equivalent of "Mr." Then there were the various guilds of goldsmiths, carpenters, tailors, butchers, stone cutters, jewelers and other craftsmen who tended to concentrate in certain cities, or sections within the cities, which became famous on that account. Kutahya, for example, was well-known for its artisans in ceramics. Finally there were the rest, those who had no identifiable skill and held menial jobs, among them the men who had come to Istanbul from the interior of Turkey to get away from unendurable repression and poverty. These were the *bantoukhd*s whose days and nights were often spent entirely in the streets, in public buildings, or at the servants' quarters or doors of the rich, at the latter's beck and call. Sympathetic creative writers romanticized them to some extent.

Only one thing was necessary to qualify as an amira: Money. Those among the amiras who lost their wealth fell from grace. As a group they thought alike and financed nearly all of the enterprises of the Armenian community, schools and hospitals included. The Patriarchate's other income was whatever people put in the collection plates during church services, which was not much. There was often a willing cooperation between the patriarch and the amiras, partly because the patriarch knew that the amiras could remove him from office without much difficulty. In 1842 Sultan Abdulmejid decided to create a Treasury of the Ottoman Empire. (Up to that time each minister of the Sultan had his own "bank" and ran his ministry with more or less financial independence.) The board of Abdulmejid's Treasury was composed of twelve bankers. They were all Armenians, all twelve of them. It follows that the cause of the Armenian genocide less than a century later was not Islam or even Turkishness, but the corruption of these by racism, of which nationalism is a milder form—often not so mild in itself.

The Patriarch of Constantinople received his secular power not from the people, but from the Sultan, who knew only one way of granting power to someone—creating a mini-clone of himself. The way the patriarch exercised power among his people seemed of a similar pattern with the manner in which the sultan ruled the empire. The patriarch could imprison his subjects for infractions of the law; he could even deliver the offender to the Ottoman authorities for capital punishment. He also had the power to prevent the publication of anything that did not meet with his approval. Nor is it by coincidence that there were efforts to curtail the authority of the patriarch and of the amiras at a time when the sultans themselves were more or less forced to make concessions to the more vociferous of Turkish leaders who became impatient with a despotic monarchy and its economic and political consequences at home and abroad.

Sultan Abdulmejid's *tanzimat* (perestroika) proclaimed in his *hatti sherif* (noble decree) of Gulhane (the rose chamber) in November 1839, promised equality before the law to all the citizens of the Ottoman Empire regardless of race or religion. The decree was composed by Mustafa Reshid, the Sultan's ambassador to London, when he, the Sultan, was a boy of sixteen. In 1846 the Ministry of Education was instituted, freeing the Empire from the scholastic monopoly of the ulama. Seventeen years after the *hatti sherif*, in 1856, the *hatti humayun* (imperial decree) of Sultan Abdulaziz reaffirmed the human rights of the minorities, Christians in particular. The nineteenth century *tanzimat* was certainly politically motivated and may not have been a genuine effort at reform. But that does not change its impact on the population. Only one year after the *hatti humayun* the Armenian National Constitution or Bylaws (*Azcayin Sahmanatrouthyoun*) was being submitted to the Sultan for approval. At the same time a secret committee of progressive Ottomans was at work in Constantinople with the aim of further limiting the Sultan's power.

The liberal, presumably progressive attitudes were associated with nationhood, while the more conservative attitudes, being old, were associated with that ancient institution, the church. Then, as the freethinking notions prevailed, the church itself became predominantly an institution serving nationalistic aspirations. The main aim of the Armenian

National Constitution was to limit the power of the patriarch and of the amiras. *Sahmanatrouthyoun* literally means "setting of limits." Its redaction and adoption were not a smooth process. The quarrels were bitter, on occasion violent, between the lay leaders of a national assembly on one hand, and the patriarch and his supporters on the other. Power was wrested from the patriarch and from the amiras, but not without a fight. As Marxism teaches, power is never given. It is always taken.

The Ottoman (Osmanian) Empire had been created late in the thirteenth century by Sultan Osman I Gazi. It ended in 1923 when Mustafa Kemal Pasha laid what he thought would be the foundations of a westernized, progressive, secular nation-state. It is this nation-centered policy, following as it did the genocidal decimation of the Armenian people, that deprived the Patriarchate of its former stature. Thus the situation changed again, again to the detriment of the Armenian Church in Turkey. A process which had its origin in the earlier decades of this century came to its conclusion in 1960, just one year before the election of Patriarch Shnork, when the *Azcayin Sahmanatrouthyoun* which had regulated Armenian collective life in Turkey (and later in the Diaspora) was formally made null and void.

The neighborhood of the Patriarchate at 20 Sarapnel Sokak was at one time a posh district where amiras had their homes. It has deteriorated. Only paces away to the south of the building is a section of narrow, crowded streets lined with shops, their merchandise spread out on the sidewalk. The articles on sale are shiny and shoddy. Many of the shops are restaurants or fast food joints where the food and the smell are—well, no more pleasant than in any comparable section of any large metropolis anywhere in the world. Shabbily dressed pedestrians run for safety to the sidewalk whenever a car or a bus passes by, for the vehicle takes up the entire width of the street. Once I noticed a group of children playfully chasing each other. I asked a companion if they were Armenians. These two are, those three are not, he said. He had a way of knowing.

Only the first two floors of the Patriarchate are used today as offices. Patriarch Shnork lived on the third floor where he had his bedroom, library, living and dining rooms, and a guest room. In view of the known predilections of other high-ranking clergymen, and since Patriarch Shnork himself controlled the funds of the Patriarchate, one would expect his living quarters to be a bit more opulent. They were in fact noticeably plain. The water in the bathroom was heated only when someone took a shower, to save on gas. Dikin Makrouhi and Dikin Payloun, two most amiable sisters who were always willing to go out of their way to make a guest feel at home, assisted by a third woman, bought the groceries, cooked, made coffee, and saw to it that the place was kept neat and clean.

Across the hall from the modestly furnished room that the Patriarch occupied there is a small chapel for His Beatitude's personal devotions and occasional services for the staff. I meant to—but did not—ask whether the chapel was Archbishop Shnork's own idea. I thought it remarkable at any rate that an Armenian bishop, in this day and age, should have a place set aside for prayers at his own residence. On this floor also is the room of the Rev. Manuel Vardapet Yergatian, who was an assistant to Patriarch Shnork. Three large tanks of tropical fish occupy a good portion of this room, adding an element of joy to the life of Father Manuel, which has not been easy, particularly during the years of his imprisonment, in harsh conditions, on charges that have proved false. There is no trace of bitterness in him. He is witty, knowledgeable, energetic, always ready to be of assistance. He is seen working during the late hours of the night, and up at or before dawn.

One of the offices on the lower floor is that of K. Pamboukjian, a member of the Turkish Academy, the historian of the Patriarchate and the author of many articles and biographies of patriarchs. All of the offices are sparsely furnished. The desks are old, the wooden chairs and benches bare. The woodwork in the interior of the building appears to be a relic of bygone affluence. The exterior of the building is grey with horizontal stripes of darker grey. It was being repainted during our stay there, in June 1989, for the first time since 1966.

The municipality of Istanbul has appropriated and demolished the Armenian "Jerusalem house" nearly adjacent to the Patriarchate, and built on the lot a residence for the city police. (The Jerusalem House was one of the buildings that were put up by way of assisting in Istanbul the brotherhood of the Armenian Monastery of Jerusalem. The larger aim was to show solidarity between the two Patriarchates, and heal the damage caused by antecedent quarrels. The building was not usable when the city took it over and bulldozed it—revealing beneath its foundation Armenian and other objects of archaeological interest. Built in 1833, the building belonged, in principle at least, to the Patriarchate of Jerusalem.) There is a mosque almost across the street in the back of the Patriarchate. A stentorian muezzin sings through a loudspeaker five times a day inviting the Moslem faithful to prayer.

Across the narrow street, which widens a bit just in front of the Patriarchate, stands the Armenian Church of the Holy Mother of God (*Sourp Asdwadzadzin*). This was originally a small chapel built within 40 days, as the regulations required, in 1610, on a lot that was previously a Greek cemetery. It has the distinction of being the only church west of Cilicia, where a catholicos was consecrated—Garabed of Oulnia (Zeytoun), the first and last catholicos consecrated in Constantinople (1726 AD). Patriarch Hovhannes Golod, who wielded more authority than the Catholicos, saw to it that the pitiable, chaotic conditions then prevailing in Armenia did not become worse with the see of Etchmiadzin unoccupied.

The Chapel of the Holy Resurrection, on the northern side of the Church of the Holy Mother of God, now serves as a hall of sorts, while the stately Church of the Sons of Thunder (*Vortvots Vorodman*), on its southern side, is for the time being completely abandoned. There are some rooms over the complex where the Patriarchate houses refugees from the Turkish provinces. There were, in June, two such families left. From what one could see of them the conditions in which they lived were not enviable.

In the gloomy half-dark of the depleted interior of the Church of the Sons of Thunder a visitor can make out the bare altars and other remnants of a once great house of worship. Pigeons fly in and out of its various apertures. They have found convenient locations for nests. Standing in the middle of this desolation a visitor might recall a singular event, an event that occurred right here, inside this very building:

It is Sunday, April 11, 1820. The *badarak* is in progress. Several Armenian *Catholic* priests, wearing the *veghar* and the *pilon* (two vestments proper to the clergy of the Armenian *Orthodox* Church) are actively participating in the celebration. What are they doing here? They are present as proof of the success of 15 years of negotiations, of which this celebration of the Divine Liturgy together is a culmination, demonstrating that the Armenian Catholics and the Armenian Orthodox have reunited.

Half of the congregation are Armenian Catholics who have never set foot in this church before. Uncommon things happen as the celebration proceeds: the addendum to the Creed, traditionally attributed to Saint Gregory the Enlightener, is not recited by the celebrant. The names of Hovhannes Vorodnetsi and of Movses and Krikor Datevatsi, three of the better known champions of Armenian orthodoxy, appear to have been struck from the dyptichs. Patriarch Boghos uses the occasion to ordain two deacons to the priesthood, and he does *not* ask them whether they abjure the Council of Chalcedon, the rejection of which Council almost gives the Armenian Church its identity! Many in the congregation note the changes with satisfaction. A fitting thing to do, they think, a small price to pay for the ecclesiastical oneness of the Armenian people in Constantinople, and eventually everywhere. Others on both sides of the reuniting parties are deeply upset. They were opposed to any concession to "the other side" and now they bristle with anger. They see the reunion as a rejection of their faith, of the tradition that makes them who they are . . .

Following that extraordinary *badarak* of 1820 the Armenian Catholic community of Constantinople was to place itself under the jurisdiction of the patriarch. The patriarch in turn would make certain terminological modifications in the relevant documents or services of the Orthodox to assure the Catholics that the reunion did not entail a denial of their basic doctrines. It did not work out. Those elements of the Armenian community, on both sides of the fence, who were dead set against reunion prevailed.

It did not work out partly because it had political undertones with which the Sultan's men were not pleased. But there was here something more than the failure of an attempt at reunion. The failure was symptomatic. It showed the major trends of the nineteenth century. Armenianism was gaining over Armenian Christianity. An Orthodox/Catholic reunion would have been the realization of an ecumenical, Christian, that is, *religious* achievement. But religion no longer defined collective self-consciousness. Within four months of the formal reunion unruly crowds marched on the Patriarchate chanting: "We are Armenians! We are Armenians! We will not be frankified!" Discontented Catholics too spread false rumors designed to kill it. Leaders of the movement were executed. Among these was Amira Krikor Sakayan, aged eighty. His severed head rolled on the pavement in front of the Church of the Sons of Thunder, across the street from the Patriarchate, on a Saturday at the hour of the evening service. Other leading prominent individuals were exiled.

Six years after that ill-fated *badarak* a fire that burned most of Constantinople also destroyed the Church of the Sons of Thunder along with everything around it. The work of reconstruction began two years later in 1828. The new complex (known in its totality as The Mother Church) was composed of six churches and chapels: The Church of the Holy Mother of God in the center, the somewhat taller Churches of the Sons of Thunder and of the Holy Cross to its south and north, with, in between, the chapels of the Nativity and of the Holy Resurrection that served to connect the main three edifices. There was, in addition, the Church of the Holy Archangels.

Of that entire complex only the Church of the Holy Mother of God is active today. Although the Patriarchate is financially in the black, and comfortably so, it still lacks the large sums that a renovation of the Church of the Sons of Thunder would require. Nor can it be surmised that the renovation, were it to be undertaken, would be easy to obtain a permit for, and that the subsequent putative use of the church would justify the effort.

To one's left, as one faces what remains of the Mother Church, is the Bezjian Mother School (*Mayr Varzharan*). Named after Amira Harouthyoun Bezjian, it has a kindergarten, primary and secondary levels, and a student body of over 250. Sinayir Yildiz is its principal.

Rarely in history have people at the upper echelons of the church hierarchy allied themselves with the poor and the weak. Nor was their chumminess with the rich and powerful due exactly to the latter's religious sensitivities. But Bezjian appears to have been genuinely pious and sincerely charitable. There does not appear to be anything self-serving, suspicious or cynical about his support of the church. He was among those exiled on the occasion of the disturbances that followed the stillborn Catholic/Orthodox reunion. He was promptly reinstated.

The Patriarchate has 16 schools in Istanbul. If we take into account the four Armenian Catholic schools, there is a total student population of over 4,000. Toward the middle of the last century, when literacy was much less prevalent, the Patriarchate had 42 schools where about 200 teachers taught close to 4,500 boys and 1,200 girls. By 1914 there were 800 Armenian schools in Turkey with a total student population of 81,000.

All the schools follow the state educational curriculum. Courses may be taught in Armenian, and Armenian may be taught as a second language. The law requires that a Turk be given a post in the administration of the school. His decisions may have to be implemented even if he is only an assistant principal.

When I asked an Armenian priest to take me to the Bezjian school, he chuckled. "I cannot," he said. No Armenian clergyman is allowed to set foot inside an Armenian school. Nor, incidentally, is any clergyman allowed to walk in the streets wearing anything that distinguishes him as a clergyman. Exceptions to this rule (which some disregard) are the heads of religious communities, the Armenian and Greek patriarchs and the chief rabbi of Turkey included. Actually the written permission that the patriarch-elect receives from the government of the Republic of Turkey to wear his clerical garb in public is the equivalent of the firman with which the Sultan recognized him during the Ottoman rule.

In the region of Istanbul the Armenian Patriarchate oversees 32 churches, including typically the Church of Saint Gregory the Enlightener at Galatya. Patriarch Shnork was fond of saying that the Galatya church "is the oldest and the newest of the Armenian churches in Istanbul." It is the oldest in the sense that it was originally constructed sixty to ninety years before the fall of Constantinople (1453 AD). The church, particularly its Chapel of the Savior of All, had been a place of pilgrimage for generations of Armenians. As a consequence it holds a very special place in the hearts of the Armenians of Istanbul, who give it a "central" importance, which is why the school connected with it is the Central School.

The reconstructed church is a cause of rightful pride, and it is impressive indeed. Its columns are covered with marble, deep rose in color. The altar is of ivory onyx. I estimated the length of the nave to be about fifteen yards. Eighteen steps lead down to the new Chapel of the Savior of All. Here, directly under the bell tower, is the tomb of Patriarch Hovhannes Golod of Paghesh, covered by its original stone. Golod was born in 1678, and was patriarch from 1715 to 1741. The three walls of his mausoleum are covered by the Goudina (Kutahya) tiles removed from the original church.

Many of the Armenians of Istanbul did not support, late in the 1950's, the expensive idea of building the new church. The argument was that it would play up the presence of the Armenian community in the city, and possibly provoke ill will. There was no point in flaunting Armenian architectural art in a very busy section of the most populous of Turkish cities. But those on the side of Patriarch Karekin, who spearheaded the project, won with the counter argument that they were adding to the beauty of a major cosmopolis on its way to modernization.

The church at Galatya is under the supervision of the Board of Supervisors of the Armenian Central School (*Getronagan Varzharan*). After a rather sparsely attended Divine Liturgy on a Thursday they were kind enough to invite Marie and me to share with them their customary luncheon. It was evident moments after the benediction (given by Father Narek Kadehjian, the parish priest who is a robust man in his late seventies) that we were in no sense strangers, but members of the family. There were even verses composed right there and then in our honor, the theme being that we should relay to our compatriots in our country the expression of their heartfelt love.

Twenty-six priests, ranging in age from 30 to 92 (median

61.88) almost all with no more than a high school education, minister to the sacramental needs of the Armenian faithful of Turkey. Among the rare exceptions to the rule is the young, energetic Father Krikor Damadian, a former pharmacist, and an expert in the medicinal properties of various herbs. He is employed at the Patriarchate while serving as the parish priest of Kadikoy.

Under the jurisdiction of the Patriarchate is the only living Armenian woman deacon, Hripsime Sassounian, 62, who now lives in Lebanon. She is the last member of her (Kalfayan) order, which means that the chances of another Armenian woman being ordained deacon are, to put it optimistically, remote. Sister Sassounian joined the order, and received her veil of celibacy in 1953 from Patriarch Karekin. A graduate of the Armenian Elementary School of Damascus, she served as the accountant of the Kalfayan School. The order had at the time four other sisters.

The Kalfayan order and orphanage (for girls) was established in 1866, by patriarchal ordinance. The founder both of the order and of the orphanage was Abbess Srpouhi Kalfayan who became a nun at age 18. She had an uncommon talent as an embroiderer, won the most coveted prizes in that art and was recognized throughout Europe. When the illustrious Bishop Nersess Varzhabedian (later Patriarch, 1874-1884) proposed that she devote herself to education and social service, she accepted in the conviction that she was to offer to God "the only talent I have." She used the contacts she had as an embroiderer, and the money she had earned to finance her institution. She also prepared, subject to the Patriarch's approval, the rules that the sisters would have to observe. She died in 1889 of diabetes. The procession at her funeral was one of the largest, if not the largest in the history of the Armenian community of Istanbul.

Sisters of the Kalfayan order were deacons or senior deacons and could in that capacity assist the priest or bishop at celebrations of the Divine Liturgy. Mother Aghavni Keuseyan received the pectoral cross from Catholicos Kevork V in 1923, and was ordained a senior deacon (*avak sargavak*) by Patriarch Mesrob Naroyan in 1933. She was followed by her sister Mariam, who was ordained a senior deacon by Patriarch Karekin Khachadourian in 1955. She is recognized as such by Catholicos Vazken in an encyclical dated January 14, 1966.

I asked Patriarch Shnork whether, following the practice of his predecessors, he would ordain women deacons. "In order to be ordained a deacon a woman must be, not just a nun, but an abbess," he said. We obviously cannot have an abbess if we do not have nuns for her to be abbess of, and he doubted whether the Kalfayan order could be revived at all.

The Patriarchate presently has two deacons who intend to become priests. One of them is a student in Germany, the other is scheduled to study in England. The Patriarchate also has a large number of other deacons who have occupations of their own and whose diaconate consists in serving during the *badarak* or singing in choirs. Their ordination is often a sort of reward, a recognition of their past services to the church as choir members or as aides to the priest in his performance of ritual functions.

Aram Ateshian, 35, is the only other vardapet in Turkey, besides Manuel Yergatian. The Patriarchate has two bishops: Shahan Svajian, 64, and Mesrob Moutafian, 34. Immediately before 1915 it had some 30 bishops in 50 dioceses. In the fifties of the last century the Patriarchate had 44 dioceses, after the loss of the Diocese of Kars in 1854. Earlier in that century, and sometimes later, the formation of a new diocese could well be a function of the authority or the determination of a bishop, or even an abbot to extend his jurisdiction over a given sphere.

As I inquired about "the next patriarch" in June of last year, the answer unanimously was, "Bishop Shahan." Then I heard comments to the effect that Bishop Shahan has invested his monies well, and that he spends a portion of his time taking care of his properties. There are other bishops in the Armenian diaspora who have the required qualifications, including those which are likely to be set by the Turkish government, for the occupancy of the patriarchal see of Istanbul, but who are not at the present time administratively connected with it.

Bishop Shahan was born in September 1926, at Uskudar. He was baptized as Simon. He received his earlier education in the schools of Istanbul and graduated from the Seminary of Jerusalem in 1954 and was ordained a priest by the then locum tenens, later Patriarch, Yeghishe Derderian, who also gave him in 1961 the rank of *Dzayrakouyn* (*"primus,"* as in *primus inter pares,* first among equals) Vardapet. In 1957 he was made the director (*dessouch*) of the Seminary of the Holy Cross (*Sourp Khach Tbrevank*) by which time he had served and taught in an Armenian school in Israel. He resigned from the Holy Cross Seminary in 1961. He subsequently taught in Armenian schools in Istanbul, and served as the chairman of the Religious Council. He traveled to Etchmiadzin in 1966 to become a bishop. He has no specific assignment, but performs sacraments and rites, and preaches on occasion in the various churches of Istanbul.

In Istanbul (as everywhere else around the world) an indication of one's wealth and social standing is the pomp and circumstance with which one (or one's child) is baptized, married, or buried. The way to enhance the pageantry on such occasions is to secure the presence of a bishop, this being Bishop Shahan more often than not. He was favored as a future patriarch principally by those, usually around his age, who are comfortable with the pattern of Armenian communal life in Istanbul as it stands. These men and women will keep things much as they are, privately convinced that the days of the Armenian community in Istanbul are numbered anyway.

\* \* \*

The two Armenian dailies of the city, *Marmara* and *Zhamanak*, are fine publications whose presses are also used for the printing of books and monographs. They keep their readers informed on Turkish and international politics (particularly when this touches the Armenians), on events in the Armenian world, and on developments in the arts and sciences. Should an action of the patriarch give rise to controversy, *Marmara* tries harder to understand his position. *Zhamanak* tends to be more secular in its outlook, and more critical. Another Armenian periodical published in Istanbul, devoted largely to the theater and other arts, is *Kooliss* (backstage). A monthly put out by the Holy Savior National Hospital completes the list of Armenian publications in Turkey today.

The hospital (*Sourp Prkich Azcayin Hivantanots*) is a comparatively vast institution of both mental and physical health care and medical research. Under the general management of Pilo Atan, who is affectionately called by some "the prime minister of the Armenians of Turkey," and is sometimes seen talking into two telephones simultaneously, the hospital serves the Armenian community, the general public, and patients whom its renown draws from abroad. In addition to being competent professionals, the physicians are well versed in Armenian culture. The newest addition to the hospital is a facility, built by a local benefactor, Sarkis Govderelioglu, where the elderly may retire while still in fairly good health to spend the rest of their lives in dignity, among caring people, in a pleasant atmosphere. "It has to be good! This is where I will retire myself," Mr. Govderelioglu says.

The Armenians of Istanbul enjoy the performances of a number of choirs or singing groups (*yerkchakhoumps*). These musical events as well as other gatherings organized by graduates of various schools, by teachers' and athletic associations, create opportunities for young men and women to meet. At the same time marriages between Turks and Armenians, though still negligible in number, appear to be on the rise. In 1940 the population of Istanbul was not quite a million. The number of Armenians then exceeded 53,000. While the total population of the city increased sevenfold since that date, its Armenian population is now, according to more or less reliable calculations, about 40,000. Patriarch Shnork estimated that "there must be" in Turkey today two million "turkified" Armenians. (His own married sister Shnorhig would have to be placed among these. Another sister of the Patriarch and a brother died in their infancy. More distant relatives live in California.)

There is no way of establishing the precise pace of the assimilation of the Armenians in Turkey. Whatever its extent it is entirely in line with the nationalistic policy of the Turkish government, as distinct from that of the Ottoman Empire. The Empire, in response partly to European influences, was itself contaminated toward the end with racism, a racism that took on religious overtones when this was deemed useful in the pursuit of such political hallucinations as a Pan-Islamic Eurasian realm. But the Ottoman Empire pursued a much smarter policy before it became the sick man of Europe. That policy, though marked by acts of fanatical brutality, did not seek to eradicate or even absorb the Christian, or Jewish or Zoroastrian minorities. Rather, it let these minorities be, so long of course as they behaved and knew their places. The Empire knew how to take advantage of any talents or virtues the people of the minorities might have.

Until the choice of Ankara in 1923 as the capital, Turkey could be said to be composed of two parts: Istanbul and the rest of the country. (This pattern also prevailed in France: Paris and the rest of it.) The cultural differences between Istanbul and the *kavar* (provinces) were quite pronounced, the natives of the former capital treating the people of the *kavar* with a distinct, though perhaps politely hidden, sense of superiority. That distinction appears still to be there, if somewhat diminished.

\* \* \*

The process of extinction appears to have reached the point of no return in the provinces. Any Armenian who could migrate to Istanbul appears to have done so already. The Patriarchate itself, with help from abroad, has been trying to salvage the salvageable; that is, promising young people.

The dream of many inhabitants of Istanbul itself is to migrate to the United States or, failing that, to Canada. Nor is this peculiar to the members of the minorities. On one occasion returning from Kinaliada, Marie and I took a taxi from one of the *iskeles* of Istanbul to Kumkapi. I remarked to the Turkish driver that even the most picturesque of American cities may not surpass Istanbul in its scenic beauty. "I understand I can move to America if someone makes a request on my behalf. Could you do that for me?" he replied. I asked why he wanted to leave. "Money, I have a wife and three kids, I cannot make ends meet driving this thing," he said, driving the thing at eighty or ninety kilometers an hour within city limits and cursing everyone on the left lane going at a more reasonable speed.

An initial impression of an interested visitor to Turkey is that the pessimists among the Armenians here are right and that their community must be written off as a significant element in the composition of the Armenian diaspora. Their extinction seems to be only a matter of time, and a relatively short time at that.

The people of the Armenian diaspora—along with their leaders—perceive their co-nationals in Turkey as impermanent, and so treat that community with what may be described as benign neglect. Contributions were made in recent times to the Patriarch's various projects, including sending promising youths to study abroad, but foreign philanthropists have not invested heavily in the future of Turkish Armenians. Prominent Armenians do visit the Patriarchate, but not often. His Holiness Vazken I, who studied in Istanbul (at the Mesrobian school of Kedik Pasha) as a youth, returned there once since, to preside over the funeral of Patriarch Karekin, on July 7, 1961.

The Armenians remaining in Turkey evince interest and a measure of emotional involvement in what goes on elsewhere in the Armenian world, and they help when they can. (Forty-two tons of foodstuff and 17 tons of medicines were sent to Armenia to help the victims of the December 7 earthquake.) Yet they are on the whole rather silent spectators. Common notions that fire the enthusiasm of the Armenians around the world often have to do with claims against Turkey, and the Armenians living there cannot very well chime in. There are also no admixtures of new elements into their community. Rare must be the individual, if such exists at all, who is anxious to become a Turkish citizen. Nevertheless, the view that the Armenian community of Turkey is finished may be an inaccurate assessment of the actual state of affairs.

One must understand that there is no room in Turkey for open expressions of Armenian nationalism, or of any nationalism other than Turkish. There is no terrain available, so to speak, for the growth of non-Turkish nationalistic aspirations. Even in the meager amount of Armenian literature and drama produced in Istanbul, there are few traces of nationalistic sentiments. What will hold the community together? What vision shall propel it toward the future? Is there even a need for leaders?

Is the community condemned to watch itself fade away?

No! is the emphatic answer of a small number of young men and women. They look upon the restrictions within which they have to operate as challenges, perhaps even blessings in disguise. They can live with the limitations imposed by the government while taking full advantage of what the law does permit. It is quite possible for Turkish-Armenian citizens, they claim, to maintain a perfectly genuine Armenian identity. I talked with Bishop Mesrob Moutafian. "We made him a bishop at a rather early age, but now he thinks he, as a bishop, is our equal in all things," Archbishop Shnork had said of him, in a mild tone of fatherly annoyance.

The Patriarch's judgment is a reflection of Bishop Mesrob's impatience with the status quo. He is particularly worried about the educational level of the priests in Turkey, and the possibility of waste and abuse in the financial affairs of the Patriarchate. People are not future-oriented. Look at the Greeks, he says. They are much fewer in number, but far more active. The way things are, the Patriarch is accountable to no one, and even those elections that can be held are not held, he says. He believes the Patriarchate has close to five hundred million Turkish liras ($250,000). He reminds his interlocutors that the police residence next door to the Patriarchate was the "Jerusalem House." We did not *have* to lose it, he says.

Bishop Mesrob supports his complaints with facts and figures, which he feels confirm his belief that the Armenian community of Istanbul is not a lost cause. He himself, deeply aware of his responsibilities as a prince of the church, is a cleric of boundless enthusiasm. He is also a workaholic. Having studied in the United States, at Oxford and at the Hebrew University of Jerusalem, he is enrolled at the Angelicum University of Rome and is writing a dissertation toward a doctorate in ecumenical theology on the life and work of Hovhannes Chamourjian (Deroyents), a nineteenth-century man of notable erudition, known principally for his defense of Christian traditional doctrines against Protestant tenets. Bishop Mesrob knows Hebrew among other languages. He has been in charge of the Armenians of the Princes' Islands since July of 1988.

These islands, ten miles southeast of Istanbul, were called Princes' Islands from Byzantine times because they were places of exile (or worse) for those who had offended the emperor. "I like to put the apostrophe before, rather than after the *s*, and think of them as *The Prince's* Islands," Bishop Mesrob says, hoping his guest will catch on. The

Prince he has in mind is Christ the Lord.

We are on Kinaliada, in a four-room apartment on the second story of a building that the parish council has built as a residence for the bishop and for various church functions. The island is named Kinali because of the *kina* (henna), reddish-orange, hue of its soil. The bishop's residence is across the street from a house that Patriarch Shnork used as a summer home. His Church of Saint Gregory the Enlightener, originally built at a time in the middle of the nineteenth century when the Armenians in large numbers began to inhabit the island, is open at least in the summer seven days a week with programs for people of every age.

Bishop Mesrob points out a playground near his church. "This was a cemetery," he says. "Imagine all this area condemned because of two graves! Did you see the graves at their new location? We succeeded in obtaining the permits necessary to have them transferred so as to utilize this space for our children. It was not easy." Then he adds thoughtfully: "Sure, there are hindrances. But where there is a will there is a way. We must face the future with faith and with courage." Our visit with him was at a time when Bishop Mesrob had requested of Patriarch Shnork and the religious council that two young protodeacons whom he had trained and educated be promoted to full deacon. The candidates had received no-nonsense instruction in matters both of theory and of practice. Should they fail the required tests, they would have to wait until properly qualified.

Bishop Mesrob is as earnest in his private conversations as in his homilies. He preaches his sermon at the canonically indicated time in the Divine Liturgy, that is, at the conclusion of the synaxis and before the offertory. He does not have to postpone it, for at that early part of the service the church is already full.

The subject of his sermon on that June Sunday when we heard him for the first time was the function of the clergy, particularly high-ranking clergy. Among his listeners was the

Patriarch. Bishop Mesrob identified that function as service, humbly rendered by way of helping the faithful reach their promised eternal destiny. Compared to sermons by Armenian clergy in the United States it was rather long. He developed his theme as he proceeded. It was a good sermon, carefully thought out. One listener came away with the perception that he was using the occasion to lecture the Patriarch. Some people consider him arrogant, and there are those, inevitably, who say that he is a secretly ambitious cleric. That is not the impression Bishop Mesrob makes on a visitor.

Bishop Mesrob, who also does his share in making the presence of the Armenian Church felt in ecumenical circles in Turkey and elsewhere, is both leader and symbol to that small number of younger men and women in Istanbul who refuse to view the future of the Armenians of Turkey with pessimism.

Manuel Vardapet works in that same spirit. He has translated into Turkish some basic prayers and engages in much needed missionary work. He preaches the Gospel to Armenians wherever he finds them, and to anyone else who is willing to drop in and listen. On a Thursday in June the topic of a presentation to a mixed audience was the divinity of Christ.

Father Manuel is also an artist and craftsman. He expresses some of his devotion repairing or restoring old ecclesiastical articles and painting icons in the traditional Armenian style. The ability to fix things can be described as a sort of physical intelligence, which he surely has. Incidentally, Patriarch Shnork himself kept a box of tools in his room, and I was told he could use them deftly.

Can we then believe that the cloud of Armenian hopelessness in Turkey has a silver lining? The young clergy, men and women I referred to, are sensitive to their own collective identity in terms of their faith, the Christianity of their forefathers. This is surely reinforced by the non-Christian context in which they live and work.

Loyalty to and grateful recognition of their ancestry are reinforced in Armenian children at Kinaliada's summer "camp." It is a learning and recreation center for children mainly from the Karagozyan Orphanage (which is no longer an orphanage, but a *nakhagrtaran*, "prep school," with a student body of over 100). We walk up to the camp and climb its stairs for a chat with its director, Jacqueline Ermen, a competent, enthusiastic, vivacious woman, proud of the progress the camp has been making from year to year, in its facilities, and especially in imparting to young Armenians a sense of the richness of their culture. She introduces to us some of the students who have already arrived. She is gratified by their recitations in Armenian. She informs us that everything is nearly ready for the children who will be coming the next day. A few are already here. They are doing odd jobs. We take a brief tour of the place. The rooms are well-lighted, well-ventilated, clean. The kitchen has a number of modern appliances. It is clear from the contents of a refrigerator that the children will be fed well. We are served the customary coffee on our return to an area adjacent to the principal's office. Mrs. Ermen's optimism is contagious. As she speaks of what the camp does now and of its potential we are motivated to help. We want to make a financial contribution, which becomes something of a problem. To whose name may the check be written? Neither the camp, nor the school of which it is an extension, is a legal entity. A way is found.

Diana Kamparosyan is a youthful, smartly dressed, knowledgeable woman, who is on Kinaliada to rest and to help prepare for the arrival of the children. She is aware that Bishop Mesrob had suggested to us that we visit the Greek monastery on the highest point of the neighboring island of Buyukada. We inquire about the schedule of the ferry that goes there. Mrs. Kamparosyan offers to be our guide.

The short ferry ride from Kinali to Buyukada is most pleasant on that sunny day on the blue waters of the Marmara. As we disembark we begin to miss the breeze. We pass by a kiosk. In its window prominently displayed is a shiny coffee-table book on Israel. It occurs to me that Turkey is the only Middle Eastern nation besides Egypt that recognizes that country. I assume the friendship is mutually beneficial. As we reach the plaza Mrs. Kamparosyan's expert eyes spot the best buggy available. She talks to the driver. She specifies the route he is to follow to and from the Greek monastery. She is aware of the cost, and how far up the hill the man and his horses are able to take us. We must walk from there on.

It is a steep, narrow road uphill. I see in my imagination the penitents of old who must have walked to the sanctuary on their knees. We talk of other matters. Mrs. Kamparosyan tells us that when her husband died she did not know the difference between plastic and glass. But then she had to run the firm. She is now an executive and deals in all sorts of plastic goods. She confirms my guess that it must be a very competitive business. We talk about national affairs and the problems of the Patriarchate. She wishes there were better cooperation among the various people and elements of the community. She appreciates Bishop Mesrob's orientation toward the future.

The sun is almost directly overhead. The incline soon becomes merciless. I look for a shade where we could perhaps rest a while, but the trees around us are small and sparse. The monastery is now in plain view. As I look back—seeking encouragement from the distance already covered—I see a stocky man, wearing a necktie which he has loosened, and a jacket. He has a large handkerchief in his right hand. Walking beside him is a laborer in dusty clothes. It is obvious that the man who is now wiping the sweat off his forehead is trying to catch up to us.

"I heard you speak Armenian," he says in Armenian. He is a contractor who is renovating the monastery. He walks with us the rest of the way. I ask him about the cost of the repair at such an elevation, in such an isolated area. "Very difficult. The transportation. Very expensive. They want to fix it, they pay me, I do it," he says. They have to bring some of the material by boat and pull it up an escarpment.

The old monastery, built on several levels, has an intricate architecture. In one of the rooms being renovated I can see classical-looking Byzantine frescoes through a cloud of chalk particles. They are not covered. In front of the main church a rooster and a couple of hens are pecking at the ground for things to eat. A dog looks at us, but has obviously seen too many tourists to show any interest. There is a single priest on the premises. He is wearing creaseless black trousers. Part of his white undershirt, yellowed at the armpits, has slipped out of his trousers, exposing a large almond-shaped surface of hairy skin. He looks overworked what with the repairs and all. He does not produce the impression of being the sort of man who would or could answer questions about the history of the monastery.

As we enter the church we find two European tourists there. Some of the more interesting paintings are on the iconostasis. It is cluttered with icons of all sizes and all manner of religious artifacts, some old, some recent. There are silver heads, eyes, hands, feet, carefully placed on holy images. It is evident that people have always come here in search of a cure for their sundry ailments.

The priest eventually walks in. The Europeans begin at once to question him in German, then in French. He turns to us and asks in Turkish if we can help. Mrs. Kamparosyan graciously offers to interpret.

On the way back to the ferry we take the scenic route, the hills of the island on one side, the sparkling sea on the other. Cars are prohibited on the islands and, in order to keep the streets clean, regulations require that a basket be placed behind every horse. There are baskets behind the horses of our carriage too, but the driver reaches over and empties them into the street as soon as either of the animals relieves himself, breaking the law to spare his customers any discomfort.

As we enter the town I marvel at the manner in which the horses sense every signal of the driver and make the sharp turns required by rather narrow streets. We stop at the home of friends, Mr. and Mrs. Iskenderoz, whom we had met in Istanbul. We sit in the balcony of their apartment. The conversation turns on the old leadership, set in its ways, and the few individuals of the new generation, trying not to be discouraged by the magnitude of the job ahead. I venture the opinion that to try to reconcile the two sides or attitudes would be futile. The best that can be hoped for is the removal of animosities. The disagreements are perhaps only in the means toward a common objective. Well, maybe. It is at any rate a good, informative, witty conversation, while the lunch, with its cucumbers and other cool vegetables, is most welcome.

On an afternoon of leisure at the Patriarchate's library I asked a young man how he coped with the downside of living in Turkey. Didn't he feel hemmed in by the fact that certain opportunities are closed to the members of minorities? "Armenian boys born in the United States can dream of becoming President," I said, and pointed out that one such boy had already made it to governor. "You, because you are an Armenian, cannot become even a policeman, let alone vali. Don't you feel . . . well, held back?" The young man was there with two friends. They were all members of a group that meets regularly for Bible study and meditation. None of them was drawn enough by materialistic glitter to want to move to America.

"True," he said. "Some doors are closed against us. But that does not put us in a strait jacket. We have our identity in Christ as He has come to us in Armenian Christianity. That is our freedom. There are some careers we cannot pursue, but what does that matter? Lots of things we want to do we can do." It occurred to me to ask the young men if they had girl friends, but I did not, fearing they might find the question frivolous or an invasion of their privacy. This was a different culture and these men had other concerns as they faced their own and their community's future. Knowing what I did professionally, they asked me about miracles. Did I think them possible? Did it make good sense to expect Christian ministers to heal not only the soul, but also the body?

Someone told me, "We have no intention of coming to you Americans with hat in hand. We do not wish to beg. We should be able to generate our own monies for our own needs. And what we need is a generation of truly religious, educated, spiritually motivated clergymen. What we need are missionaries, not people who know the craft of priesthood and are in it for security, but people who know the art of finding 'the lost sheep' and who find them in order to return them to the fold." I also talked to a clergyman who said, "If I had any brains I would not have chosen this profession. I would not advise anybody to go into it. Not here."

Those who, the enthusiasms of some younger men notwithstanding, lean toward pessimism about the renewed vitality or even survival of the Armenian Church or community in Turkey may have a point. Consider the fact that a priest, Father Varak Beylerian, born in 1919 and ordained at age 59, is, all by himself, in charge of all the churches and communities in all of Turkey outside Istanbul, Iskenderun and Kirikhan. There are 16 such churches and communities, and they are spread from one end of Anatolia to the other. How many individuals all told? Fewer than three hundred, many, perhaps most, of them apparently in the second half of their lives. Do any of them know who Vartan Mamigonian is? I came away with reasons to doubt. Father Varak holds services once or twice a year at the once glorious Church of Saint Gregory the Enlightener of Kayseri, with few if any at all attending. The purpose: To prevent the authorities from taking the church over as abandoned property.

The pilgrimage to which Patriarch Shnork invited us was the sixth organized by His Beatitude since 1969. Some 70 of us accompanied him in two large buses most of the way, he himself traveling in a private minibus with his retinue. The minibus followed on occasion an itinerary of its own to visit places that were of special interest to the Patriarch, such as his birthplace.

Marie and I traveled in one of the two large buses. As "the American guests of the Patriarch" we were accorded preferential treatment all along the way, always, for example, occupying the front seats to the right of the driver. Also from the United States joining the pilgrimage was Barbara Kiredjian Lorincie. There were four other pilgrims from countries other than Turkey.

Most of the pilgrims were from Istanbul, many of them born in one or the other of the cities we were to visit along the way. With us was Father John, a splendid Catholic priest attached to the bishopric of Istanbul, who taught English to some of the staff of the Patriarchate and learned Armenian in the process. At one point during our tour a Turkish newspaper noted in a brief article the odd presence of this Englishman among a group of Armenian pilgrims. What was *he* doing here? Might his concern be something other than pilgrimage? There were those who observed that, interestingly enough, the question was raised the day after the British Parliament abrogated an existing accord with Turkey and decided that Turkish citizens could not enter England without a visa.

Kayseri is the first major city the pilgrims visited. Before World War I this was a diocesan center with its Armenian monastery, a convenient place where the Patriarch of Constantinople could dispatch rivals or troublesome clergymen, ostensibly for a "retreat." Kayseri was big enough for the exiles not to be unduly resentful or overly inconvenienced, and far enough from Istanbul for the offending clergymen to be out of the patriarch's way altogether. The present population of the city is about 300,000, with perhaps one Armenian for every hundred thousand.

Of the Armenians now living in Kayseri one is a toothless old woman who wears a black *izar* (or *chadder*, as the Persians call it, but without a veil). If she is a little odd, it is because destiny has not been kind to her. She is, at any rate, full of energy and utterly fearless. When I tried to engage her in conversation in the courtyard of the Armenian church she wrathfully pointed to the remains of a staircase that still hung tenaciously onto an exterior wall of the church—with bare mortar jutting here and there from between the stones—and led nowhere. "They have destroyed everything, everything! They have built nothing!" she screamed as if wanting to be heard by the whole world.

The second Armenian in Kayseri is an old man, presumably the warden of the church grounds. He does not have very much to do in that capacity, does not seem to be with it, in fact, and says very little. The third is an illustrious young man, whom we all came to know within hours of our arrival, referring to him affectionately as *Khent* ("crazy") Sarkis. He flaunts his Armenian name (I heard he has it tattooed on his forearm), claims he is related to the Gulbenkians (who were indeed from Kayseri) and runs a tavern with a Turk to whom he refers as his partner. When Sarkis was there, no one else was in charge.

At an evening church service in Kayseri Patriarch Shnork bid the congregation to prepare for the next day's *badarak* with abstinence and meditation. We were there, after all, as pilgrims. That same night all of us, or at least those of us who did not mind paying 20,000 liras (about ten dollars) for the announced feast, repaired to "Sarkis's place." There we ate all manner of meat, drank quantities of raki, listened and danced to Turkish music late into the night.

When I saw Sarkis for the first time he was wearing a white suit with a double-breasted jacket over a white shirt unbuttoned half way down, revealing a strong, sun-burned chest. His shoes, also white, were high-heeled. He is a tall, muscular, lean man with thick black hair, dark, penetrating eyes. One can almost read on his forehead the warning, "Don't mess with me!" He has been in and out of jails a number of times, partly because he won't let anyone forget he is an Armenian, someone told me. I asked him why he was not married. "The perfections I am looking for I can't find in any one woman," he said. He also said that he would like to die young so his corpse would look nice. When a pilgrim said something in Armenian, he protested: "Speak Turkish so we too can understand something!"

It was Sarkis who deftly cut the throats of three sheep after they had been blessed in front of the Church of Saint Gregory the Enlightener, to be offered sacrificially. The animals shook spasmodically even as their blood was forming a surprisingly large pool a few feet away from the church wall. A Turkish reporter took a picture of the slaughter. Many pilgrims were not happy with the ceremony and a passionate discord broke out. Voices rose in protest. The custom was "primitive!" "barbaric!" "Christians should not be doing such things!" someone shouted in nearly uncontrollable anger. "Actually it's a *tajik* custom," another said also with indignation. A listener agreed with the spirit of the remark, but tried to correct the mistake that we had inherited the practice from the *tajiks*. In the absence of the Patriarch no one knew very much about the history of the practice. To Sarkis all the ado was about nothing. He informed the audience that he had learned the art of killing sheep while still a boy, watching his dad.

The entrance to the courtyard of the Church of Saint Gregory is on a narrow, neglected road lined with unkempt dwellings. Inasmuch as this is a public institution the Turkish flag flies over the low, small entrance. On our way there on Sunday morning some of the pilgrims recognized many of the houses built and owned by prominent Armenians decades ago. People from Sivas were with us, having provided the wherewithal for our Sunday meal—the sheep butchered the day before. Several men were already milling about in the churchyard as we arrived. The *badarak* was in progress.

The altar, with decorative half columns on both sides, and a painting of the Madonna and Child framed by an intricate ornamental openwork, appears to be neatly adorned, but impoverished otherwise. The vestments and the choir robes brought from Istanbul contribute to the deceptive opulence of the interior of the church. There are no benches on the floor. There never were. Benches are a western innovation. Scattered are ancient, faded rugs that have lost their pile. Some have holes. There is a certain greyness about everything other than the altar and some of the clothes worn by the members of the congregation. Here and there people have formed small groups and are having hushed fellowships of their own, quite unmindful of the Liturgy that is being celebrated by His Beatitude. But that disinterest does not characterize the congregation as a whole. Many are deeply involved in the common worship. There is something other-wordly about the expressions on their faces.

My eyes follow a venerable Armenian woman entering the church. She is wearing an old, long dress of mute colors with a knit jacket over it. A large unmatching shawl covers her head, with grey to white strands of hair trickling out of it. Why do I watch her with such fascination? Am I not here to worship? She leaves her shoes at the gate, puts a lira or two in the plate, helps herself to two tapers and heads for the picture of the Mother of God hanging on the wall of an apse to the left of the altar. The picture is under glass. (That's unusual. As I later look closely, I see that someone has tried to erase the beard and mustache that a native hooligan must have added to disfigure this antique Christian icon. The glass is there to protect the picture against further vandalism.) The woman presents her petitions to the Mother of God, plants one of her tapers in the box before the image (she will use the other taper during the service for the repose of souls), and moves down to a spot in the nave that is covered with a tattered kilim. She crosses herself slowly, and is lost to this world. My eyes move to an elderly man. He is there, prostrate, forehead touching the floor. He will surely remain in that position of deep adoration for a long time. Whence does this woman, whence does this man, inherit this faith? How far into their history must one trace the devotion they are demonstrating here today? To the first converts of the Apostle Thaddeus who brought the Light of the World to Armenia? If, I reflect, the entire enterprise of coming here, to this distant church to celebrate the Divine Liturgy—if the Patriarch's determination to undertake all the hardships of this pilgrimage gives this woman and this man the opportunity of entering into communion with the God of their Fathers, in the church of their immediate ancestry, in this public worship, then it needs no further justification. Their participation, and the participation of others like them, saves the Divine Liturgy from being some sort of an opera.

Patriarch Shnork preached the sermon. It was, appropriately, on the life, consecration, and mission of Gregory the Enlightener, and the contemporary significance of his work. He displayed on this as on other occasions a feeling for the nature and amount of hope that it made sense to try to impart to his audience. His own notable mastery of the Armenian language notwithstanding, mindful of the capacity of his average listener, he never used a fancy word.

The time came for communion. The Patriarch was distributing it on his knees, on the bema. A woman approached the chalice. Some men happened to be waiting behind her for their turn. Another woman who was standing on the side seized the first woman by the arm, pulled her forcefully away: "The men first!" she said, loud enough to be heard by everyone. The women waited until the last male person had partaken of the Body of Him Who had come to proclaim the equality of all people as children of God.

The *madagh* (sacrificial meal) was eaten on this day, June 11, after the *badarak*. Patriarch Shnork, several of the men from Sivas, and the more enterprising of the pilgrims sat at the long table in the courtyard. Unlike the food which was abundant, places to sit were at a premium. One boy and one girl, both about twelve, took turns after the meal to read addresses of welcome in the impeccable Turkish accent of the region. One of the children took the occasion to shower praises on Turkey, the fatherland. On duty in the courtyard were men of the militia, there for the protection of the guest and his entourage.

Kayseri, the historic Caesarea, was founded as Mazaca centuries before Christ by that legendary biblical figure to whom the fifth(?)-century Armenian historian Movses Khorenatsi refers as "our Aram." In the first century BC the city was for a time under the rule of Tigran the Great, the Armenian King of Kings. It was in Caesarea, of course, that Gregory the Enlightener was made a bishop and became the first catholicos of all Armenians in 314 AD. Caesarea was then situated about 155 miles from the frontiers of Greater Armenia. Gregory preached the Gospel on his way back to Armenia in the province of Daron, an area to the northwest of Lake Van, whose principal city was Ashdishad, and which became famous with its monastery of Saint Garabed (John the Baptist) at Moush. This monastery was probably the most popular and is the best known center of pilgrimage in recent Armenian folklore. The pilgrimage was recommended particularly to women who did not find themselves pregnant even after a year or two following their marriage.

The Turkish highways connecting the major cities of the country are well built and still in good condition. We had traveled from Istanbul to Kayseri overnight, with a stopover at a cafe-restaurant in Bolu. "You will like it. It's probably one of the best of its kind in the country," a friend had said. Cool night air, good food, efficient service.

Our buses had entered Kayseri on a four-lane avenue lined with shops and apartments. Adding to the color of the apartments was laundry hanging on lines in the balconies. The buildings, already deteriorating here and there, gave the impression of having been put together hastily. The hotel where we were taken would not earn stars from the American Automobile Association, though we missed even *its* comfort and cleanliness when we subsequently stayed at one or two inns in other cities.

Since childhood I have associated the name Kayseri with three things: the hanging gardens of ancient Caesarea, the business acumen of its people, and good beef. The hanging gardens are of course gone, but flowers are not an uncommon sight. The business acumen of the people I assume is still there. The *pasterma* I tasted in one of its shops was inferior to that made in various cities of the United States. In the old quarter of the city, in large pans placed on the ground, cheeses and other milk products are sold noisily. Outside the gate of the market men in their native costumes sit in long rows along the walls of the building in the plaza opposite the well-preserved remnant of a Roman citadel, conversing while they watch those who watch them. At a little distance from the plaza there is a *medrese*, a Moslem school, consisting of a large courtyard surrounded by little rooms, converted into a museum. It has a fairly good collection of Ottoman and some non-Ottoman coins. There are other pieces poorly displayed and improperly marked, if marked at all.

This part of the town contrasts with its outskirts. I saw what seemed to be a cement factory on our way in. There are also smokestacks that signify the industrialization of the city.

Near Kayseri is the Erciyas (the ancient Argaeus) Dagi, a resort area at an altitude of over a thousand meters. It is also grazing land for numerous flocks of sheep. The landscape is dotted by conical tents, identical to each other, that are slightly curved in on the sides. The white of the tents contrasts beautifully with the green of the grass. Shepherds live here at this time of the year. We are here for a picnic. A gentle breeze adds to the loveliness of the surroundings. I gaze off into distant expanses. This is Cappadocia. These are the hills and valleys trod by Basil the Great and the two Gregorys of Nazianzus and Nyssa. There were Armenians among their disciples. They gave shape to the liturgy and the theological thinking of the Armenian Church.

The picnic is over. I have an empty bottle of soda in my hand. I look around. There are no trash cans. I do not know what to do with the bottle. "This is what we do with it," a pilgrim says, as he takes it and flings it as far as he can.

Not too far from Caesarea one can visit the caves and underground dwellings—multi-level marvels of engineering—where the monks lived away from paganism, and more or less safe from persecution. Some vineyards of Cappadocia were cultivated for the wine of the Eucharist. One winery now has a dimly lit salesroom with fine oriental rugs on the floor and on the benches lined against the walls. Tourists sit on them, are given tastes of red and white wines, and buy a bottle or two on the way out. We opened our bottles back in Dayton, Ohio. Not Rothschild to be sure, but good.

A Turkish newspaper published a story while we were there, to the effect that one of the reasons why Turkey is not liked by everyone is that Turks are ignorant of their own history. (Another reason was that they do not brush their teeth.) Do they know the history of any other people? A young Turkish man who had studied in the United States had been sitting next to us on the plane on his way home. He kept talking about the expensive electronic gear he had bought in the States and was taking with him. When we told him who we are, he made a telling declaration. He sincerely, perhaps even innocently, believed that the Armenians never had a kingdom of their own or, for that matter, a culture to speak of. "Armenian" to him meant something like "gypsy."

So the Armenians living in Turkey should be grateful to the Turks for providing them with a civilization to identify with, and to be proud of. He could not comprehend that Armenians around the world should have certain claims against his country. Suppose, I reflected, just suppose we could find a way of teaching Turkish youth something of our history, but I soon abandoned the thought as a fantasy.

Probably large numbers of Armenians in Turkey, as large numbers of Armenians everywhere, do not know their own history either. In one of the cities we visit, after one of the characteristically history-oriented sermons of the Patriarch, I talk to one of the pilgrims, a woman of about forty. She is schooled. She speaks Armenian well, with no admixture of foreign words. She also speaks good French. She does not know that Sis was the capital of an Armenian kingdom, or that there was an Armenian kingdom in the region. She has never heard the name *Cilicia* before. I try not to show my astonishment. I ask someone else who Krikor Naregatsi was. "Didn't he write the Bible?" she asks. Can I blame her? I think of the Armenians around the world who have not even heard the name. This woman knows at least that there is an Armenian man named Krikor Naregatsi who has written something and that what he has written has something to do with the Bible. So what is peculiarly unsettling about the ignorance encountered here in Istanbul? A preconception, perhaps.

When I was a boy the word *bolsetsi* (an inhabitant of the *polis* or city, namely Constantinople) still carried a connotation of sophistication and culture not encountered every where—except of course when the *bolsetsi* in question was a *tulumbaji* or a *hamal*, the proverbially illiterate, crude and clever fireman-pumper or porter. The pumps these *tulumbajis* used, mounted on wheels, are now seen in museums. And there still are in Istanbul Armenian men and women of great erudition and distinct refinement. It is a pleasure to sit and talk with them, and one can only hope that there will always be people to whom they will transmit their love of learning, their drive and their grace.

At the end of a day of fellowship, of candid conversation with new friends, I ask myself this question: If a single word were required to describe the inner attitude with which an Armenian lives his or her life in Turkey, what would it be? I think it would have to be *caution*. I remember an old *Sepasdatsi* ([former] inhabitant of Sivas) telling me once that when Archbishop Torkom (Koushagian) went there before World War I as a Primate, thousands of Armenians lined the streets to welcome him, but that many were against this demonstration because they did not want the Armenian community there to be conspicuous. I recall the doubts that the people of Istanbul had about building a conspicuous Armenian church at Galatya. Are minorities endangered when they flaunt their culture and competences? Do they become too visible?

When the pilgrims visited Talas, the hilltop section of Kayseri where the well-to-do have their modern homes, the Vali of the Province granted us a brief audience outdoors. He lives in a house that was built as a gift to Ataturk, the founder of modern Turkey, who did not have the opportunity to live there; but since it was intended for him, one can readily understand the magnificence both of the structure and the location of the house. As we set foot on the premises a whispered instruction begins to circulate issuing from within our group no doubt, to the effect that we should not talk Armenian here. Not audibly. Those of us who choose to ignore the whispers are not, of course, penalized in any way, but that such a rumor should spread at all . . .

The Vali is a lean, athletic, courteous man. In his little speech he welcomes us warmly, gives explanations about the house, then graciously offers a rose from his gardens to one of the ladies in our group. Many are prompt to express their gratitude with evident sincerity.

Caution is the attitude that the circumstances of the Armenian minority in Turkey call for. It is not easy to live with the descendants of the men who decimated your ancestors. But there must be adjustment. Every Armenian in Turkey knows, often from personal experiences of outbreaks before and after World War II, that government reactions to one happening or another can be unexpectedly harsh. While one must, when wronged, invoke the laws of the land in one's favor, there is no point in engaging in provocative acts. One must be cautious. One may remind a receptive Turkish audience of some of the irregularities of the past, but one does so gently, without implying too much or pressing too hard. One may assume that not all Turks want to remain ensconced in their self-serving version of history. Many want to know the facts and base a future on a realistic estimate of the past. Still, when you speak of unpalatable truths to them, or even among trusted co-nationals, you do well to do so softly, without any show of rancor or noticeable gestures of defiance.

The seventy or so pilgrims to Van included present or former manufacturers, physicians, writers, business persons, employees, housewives. A few of the younger women were there as companions to their parents. Without them the average age would have probably stood somewhere between 55 and 60. The Patriarch traveled in his minibus with Dr. and Mrs. Garo Arman. Dr. Arman, a well-mannered, urbane individual who knows his way around in government circles, was adviser to the late Patriarch, principally in the latter's relations with the Turkish authorities. He is a practicing physician. Also in the minibus were the Rev. Aram Ateshian, a vartabed, and Rev. Muron Ayvazian and his wife.

The tour guide in one of the buses was Erdal Bey, a fine gentleman of scholarly interests, a former teacher of archaeology, and quite knowledgeable in the history of ancient Armenian monuments. The associate tour guide was a sympathetic Armenian young man, Arto, also a singer. His wife assisted him in seeing to it that everyone was back in his or her bus after a stop, and was as comfortable as possible. Arto told me that he was in the process of negotiating a contract for a tour in the United States. He sang for us in the bus and, by invitation, at Sarkis's place and other restaurants where we dined. He accompanied himself on a jingle drum.

Almost at no time did we travel in anything approaching silence. Whenever Arto was not entertaining us with his Turkish songs, the driver, often on demand, took over and played more *sharkis* on tape. After a while I found myself appreciating authentic Turkish music better than strains that were "Americanized" a la Crosby or Sinatra with a presumed appeal to the younger generation. I noticed that a young woman in our group knew every detail of the life of one of the singers. She remembered the day, hour and minute when she had the opportunity of shaking hands with him. She never tired of asking for his songs. His father (or mother, I have forgotten which) is an Armenian, she said.

Two or three Armenian songs were sung in the bus during the entire course of our journey from Istanbul to Van and back. Otherwise the Turkish songs were interrupted only by reminiscences or jokes or riddles. These were told with the help of a microphone in, as one would expect, the language of the country, to an entirely Armenian audience (except the driver) by one or the other of the members of the pilgrimage who themselves spoke fluent *bolsetsi* Armenian.

There is no point in repeating any of the jokes here. None is fit to print. I have no objection to salacious jokes so long as they project some wit. Almost all of the jokes I heard on the bus were simply gross, even indecent. Did they make others laugh? They did. It was also somewhat disconcerting that the pilgrims who uttered these vulgarities were to sing, not too long afterward, some of the holiest hymns by the finest of our religious poets.

I asked someone if it would not have been a good idea

to have a speaker on the bus tell this captive audience something about the history of the places we were visiting, instead of these riddles and things. He pondered the issue. That may not have been advisable, he said. Why? He was not sure.

Most of the people on the bus were courteous and naturally friendly. Some had edibles with them, which they shared with everyone else, walking up and down the aisle to do so. Others would come around once in a while with bottles of mildly perfumed lotions and sprinkle generous quantities in your hands for you to refresh your face—which did feel hot and beaten after hours of travel. Whenever it got too hot in the bus the driver opened the door while going at full speed. There was spontaneous dancing in the aisle whenever the music lent itself to it, which was often.

In the rare intervals when the *sharkis* and the stories and the reminiscences and the jokes abated, some serious conversation could be overheard, including references to the places we were passing by. I heard someone tell a friend that religion is a matter of faith alone, a subjective thing that has nothing to do with reason. "You believe, you believe. That's it!" this person said. In another snatch of conversation the view was expressed that our early ancestors must have come to these regions from some other part of the world. Proof: In our art motifs there are representations of lions, but there never were lions in Anatolia. Our ancestors must therefore have known about lions in their original land, wherever that was. "Now I am talking about our ancestors of prehistoric times," the speaker specified. A woman explained at one point why it is that the holy communion is distributed in such small pieces at Armenian *badaraks*. At first, she said, people ate large chunks of bread. But when more and more people became Christians bread became scarce, so they had to reduce the size of each portion. It's a matter of economy, she said. I intended to ask her for the source of this intriguing piece of information, but did not have the opportunity.

Among the cities we visited on our way to Aghtamar was Sepasdia, the Sebasteia of Roman times when it was the capital of Armenia Minor. As we drive from Kayseri in a northeasterly direction I think of Saint Gregory the Enlightener. He too after his consecration in Caesarea came to Sebasteia where he found "a great number of brethren," as the historian puts it, who were to cooperate with him in his mission to make of Armenia a Christian land. I wonder if Gregory had any room left in his heart for Mariam, his one-time wife, as he was making this journey. They had separated by mutual agreement, each to follow a religious vocation. She had become a nun. She was from Sebasteia.

Any Armenian youngster who has taken an introductory course in Armenian history will be moved toward certain associations by the name "Sepasdia." He will think of the *Karasoun Mangounk* (the 40 soldiers [of Christ]) of this city, who under Emperor Licinius, in 320, were given the choice of either freezing in a lake in winter or rejecting Christianity. They, save one, chose the former alternative. A Roman soldier was moved to take the place of the one who reneged. The story of their martyrdom, with all the attendant miracles, was indelibly impressed in the memory of Christendom, and of Armenian Christians in particular. The 40 youths have been among the most popular saints. There are a number of encomiums extolling them; a church was built in Sepasdia with 40 cupolas. Many Armenians of Sepasdia felt blessed for living on land hallowed by the Forty Martyrs; the cemetery was named after them as if to insure that the souls of the departed would join the souls of the Forty.

The tenth century was an important time in the history of Sepasdia. The Armenians had more kings then than they knew what to do with. Nearly anybody who was anybody politically or on the battlefield managed to become a "king."

In the later decades of the century, however, Armenian kings, unable to defend themselves against the various Moslem tribes attacking them from the east, entered into an ingenious arrangement with the Byzantine emperor. They would cede their territory to the emperor who would thus enlarge the empire without a fight and, moreover, have subjects who would fight for him against eastern invaders. The Armenian king would be a vassal, enjoy imperial protection—and go on ruling much as he did before, that is, autocratically. One such king was Senekerim-Hovhannes Ardsrouni, whose kingdom acceded to Byzantium's more or less nominal rule, with Sepasdia as its capital. Here he brought a piece of the Cross, whose fascinating history was woven into the history of Armenia, and which was discovered on Mount Varag by two Armenian monks named Thotik and Hovell. To house the relic Senekerim built a cathedral within a monastery at Sepasdia—the Monastery of Sourp Nshan (Holy Cross).

It was in Sepasdia that 4,000 soldiers, mostly Armenian, were preparing, in 1400 AD, to oppose the sacking of their city by Timur i Lang (Tamerlane,) the Hitler of Samarkand. Timur promised not to shed the blood of any of the 4,000 men if they surrendered. They did, and he kept his promise. He buried them all alive. Judging from what the Armenian historian of the period says of him, one of Timur's pleasures was to see little boys and girls crushed under the hooves of galloping horses. The church with the 40 cupolas was not there after Timur.

Sepasdia is the birthplace of Abbot Mekhitar, the founder of the Armenian Catholic Mekhitarist order. He was born in 1676. As an uncommon person of uncommon piety he was not simply resigned to, but accepted the poverty and pain of his eventful life. He was ordained an Armenian Orthodox priest at the Monastery of Saint Nshan at twenty. He received a license to preach and a vardapet's staff, and became a *karozich* at the church of Galatya in Istanbul. But this was a time when the Roman Catholics were active as missionaries among the Armenians, and they succeeded in winning him over. In his youth Mekhitar had had a vision of the Virgin Mary at the Armenian Monastery of Lake Sevan. She had told him that he was her adopted child, and commissioned him to be a teacher of repentance. That vision was with him all his life, notably when he founded the Armenian Roman Catholic Mekhitarist order on, as most scholars agree, September 1, 1701. Convinced that any uniquely salvation-oriented institution could not survive within the Ottoman Empire, Abbot Mekhitar took his order to Venice. No one can doubt that without the Mekhitarists modern Armenian scholarship and literature would have been considerably poorer.

It is because of such associations that the name of Sepasdia has a special resonance for Armenians. Another prominent native of the city is Taniel Varouzhan. He taught there for a time at the National Aramian School, and was paid a lira more than his colleagues because he was already recognized as one of the greatest poets of his time. He died in 1915.

"Sepasdia" had become "Sivas" by the end of the eleventh century because that is how its Turkmen conquerors pronounced it.

Estimates of the Armenian population of the region of Sivas proper immediately before the Genocide vary. A fairly accurate figure is 69,000. With its seven churches or monasteries, scores of organizations, craft associations, theater, schools, printing facilities, dailies, weeklies, political parties and religious denominations Sivas was one of the most vibrant Armenian communities in Turkey outside of Istanbul. Then one day in June 1915 all eleven Armenian neighborhoods of the city were shocked by the proclamation. The people were to be deported. It was, they were told, for strategic reasons, and for a time only. The deportees would be placed under military protection. They could take with them carts, horses and donkeys, their own or rented. Oxen-drawn wagons would be provided to those who could not afford such transportation. It is important, they were insistently told, to take along all valuables. It was safer that way. These were the instructions. Some of the Armenians, hoping against hope that there must be some truth in these declarations, cleaned their homes and worried that the doors should be securely locked while they were gone.

The orders were not so frightening. But when the time came to leave, there was nothing solicitous or gentle about their implementation. Each neighborhood was isolated and surrounded by Turkish militia. Scimitar-waving, whip-lashing roughnecks were let loose on the streets. Women and children, husbands and fathers already gone, huddled in terror, heard their menacing shrieks: "Out, infidel pigs! Out of the house and hurry! Believe us, you are finished, you will perish, you and your traitor nation, your rotten nation! We don't want your filth here or your smell. Out!"

In the meantime armed Kurdish and other gangs of bandits were being informed of the precise route the Armenian convoys were to follow.

The caravans formed. Waves of deportation surged one after the other. Arid areas were deliberately chosen to move the convoys through. They were made to rest in the middle of the night. When people sat or lay down they found themselves among corpses left behind by previous convoys. They were harried and raped; died of thirst and hunger, of heat and exhaustion. They died by drowning and by the sword. A hardy few made it to their destinations: Rakka, Deirezzor.

Viewed from the west Sivas nestles invitingly among high hills with a population today in excess of 200,000. How many Armenians among them? Thirty? Forty? Many of them accompanied us when we headed for the Armenian cemetery. Following the service for the repose of the souls of the dead, the Patriarch said in a moving address, translated simultaneously into Turkish by Deacon Shahan, that where there is no church left we must go to the cemeteries. He then spoke of the glorious Armenian cultural and religious past of Sivas. He reminded the listeners that Archbishop Torkom Koushagian, the late Patriarch of Jerusalem, who had ordained him in 1935 had been an *arachnord* of this city. He invited the Armenian subjects of the Republic to be loyal citizens and do their best to contribute to its progress. But then, he said, the authorities should not demolish our churches or allow them to perish; they should respect our cemeteries.

Live charcoals were placed on one of the graves, contained in a circle of pebbles, to burn the incense. A light breeze dispersed the fragrant smoke. The graves are few in number. Some are simply heaps of split stones. Others are made of grey cement. They are shaped like tombstones with a small cavity at the head of each, where candles can be burned protected from the wind.

"Yes, there is a church not too far from here," a pilgrim told me later, "but we are not going there. I believe the Patriarch wants to look at it. You can't get in. It is boarded." He did not know its name. He also informed me that the stones of the old cemetery—"the Cemetery of the Forty Martyrs, I believe in that direction," were stolen by natives who used them to build or renovate houses. There was no point in using stones in the new cemetery either because they too would be promptly removed.

This cemetery is at the end of a dirt road, a long distance from the center of the modern town. From here one can walk to the old cemetery. On higher ground on the left of the road there were several soldiers carrying rifles. They were looking at us curiously from the other side of a fence of barbed wire that marked the boundary of a military camp. Within this camp are the ruins of the Church and Monastery of Sourp Nshan, my companion said to me. And these are the houses, he said, pointing to a row of hovels on the right, that formed part of the Armenian quarter. I saw women watching us from dilapidated windows. Their looks were furtive and they were quite obviously very poor.

During the construction of the military camp some tombs were cut through. Human bones can be seen on the ground. I pick one up. To my untrained eye it looks like a rib. The feelings that well up within me are difficult to put into words. Perhaps I am trying to condense and relive in this one moment the life of the man or woman whose rib this is. "We are here," the Patriarch had said earlier, "in order to commune with the souls of the dead; we ourselves hope to achieve their bliss when our own remains are buried. Faith, hope and charity," he had said, and it was as if he had clarified each of these difficult concepts simply by pronouncing the words — slowly, deliberately. "When we lose these, we ourselves are lost."

As we walk to our buses and are about to leave behind us this forlorn remnant of a once dynamic Armenian city, deep from my subconscious emerge the words *Tiaki Sayle*. It is the title of a poem by Taniel Varouzhan. I used to recite it as a boy at commemorations of the Massacres. The poem is about a cart laden with the massacred, screeching its way toward the haymow of harvested saints. A thin horse pulls it. A drunken soldier trails behind. The animal's tail, brushing against the mangled bodies loaded on the cart, splashes drops of blood right and left. No one comes to weep for the dead, or to bid a last farewell . . . In the silent town only the smell of blood circulates with the zephyr . . . But in the dark, suddenly, window after window is illumined with candles, candles that pray secretly over the red pall. Then from a balcony a fair maiden in tears throws a bouquet of roses on the cart that is passing by . . .

There are some large signs along the highways of Turkey that a traveler from the West sees frequently: "How fortunate is he [or she] who says 'I am a Turk!'" I wonder. Why should a Turk be told that he or she is fortunate? It occurs to me that every country feels a desperate need to instill in its people a sense of pride and patriotism.

In the cities it is virtually impossible to spend an ordinary day without seeing somewhere or other, more than once, an image or statue of Ataturk. In Kayseri in the same plaza there are, not one, but two monuments representing him. His portrait is ubiquitous. His picture hangs on a wall of almost every room of every building where public business is transacted. The Armenian Patriarchate is no exception.

The republic Ataturk founded was to be secular. He wished to create a country that would eventually emulate the countries of the West where religion and state are separate constitutionally or otherwise. Yet in today's Turkey Moslem fundamentalism, or at least a revival of Islam, is visible or audible even to the least attentive of tourists. There are devices set up in some public places that read verses from the Koran. We did not see newly built churches, but newly built mosques or mosques under construction are not at all uncommon.

On our way to Malatya we passed through Kangal, a village known for its mineral waters. There are two pools, one for men, one for women, filled with circulating water from the springs. Little fish swim in the pools. I asked a physician in our group about the presence of fish in mineral water. His answer surprised me. "They come with the water from under the ground," he said, "and they have, as you see, a most unusual characteristic. This is unique in the world. If you have certain skin diseases, notably psoriasis, as you submerge the affected area, the fish will attack and heal it. The disease will vanish after a month's treatment. You see that the fish come in different sizes. Each has a function of its own. Some will clean around the infection, others will deliver the healing and soothing substances." A number of men were in the pool, with fish around their bodies, and it seemed to me that other fish were behind those at work, as if waiting for their turn. Several of the pilgrims took off their shoes and socks, rolled up their trousers and dipped their feet in the tepid water. They were happy when the fish came around, only to ignore them.

The region of Kangal is famous also for its dogs. They do not have to be trained, but are natural sheep dogs.

As we walked toward our buses the conversation was about the fish and the dogs, with other light talk and banter. In my own imagination the scene changed. This was the place where several Armenian convoys were assembled in 1915 before each continued on its horrid way. This is the place where self-styled officials appeared out of nowhere to take inventories of what the deportees had, "to make sure everything would be returned to you without any items missing." Many were savagely beaten to have them reveal any concealed possessions. The vaginas of women were searched for hidden jewelry. We kept on talking about the fish and about the dogs.

Yet another city where the Armenian pilgrims have a cemetery but no church to visit is Malatya, the historic Melitene, recognized by the Latins as the capital of Armenia Secunda. The Armenian cemetery of Malatya is now surrounded by various noisy shops with rumpled parts of auto bodies in and around them.

Our compatriots of Malatya, like those encountered everywhere, are generous and cordial. As we gather in the cemetery, they serve us the fruits of the season. I ask a native how many Armenians are left in the city. Maybe a little more than 20 families, he says. He repeats the word *maybe*. Before the war the *sanjak* (subdivision of a province) of Malatya had a bishop under the jurisdiction of the catholicos of Cilicia— or so the catholicos claimed. It had 43 parishes, 23 of which had churches with a membership of 20,000. There were in addition 2,000 Armenian Catholics and 1,000 Protestants.

We walk around in the cemetery. It is a lawn with large trees that shade many of the graves. I try to make out the names. I read each out loud as if to greet an unseen presence. I instinctively subtract the date of birth from the date of death. "He was a two-year-old child! He died before . . ." There was a priest available then. He prayed for his soul when they laid him here. His mother probably stood here, with flowers on the ground, on every anniversary. Perhaps more often. For how many years? Under another slab of stone, pockmarked by the passage of years, are the remains of a 73-year-old woman. I read her name, the dates. You are not dead and gone, because I am here, reading your name, I reflect, without exactly knowing what it is that I am trying to ascertain. I think of her as a child of God, probably more beloved than those whose marble mausolea are the subjects of dissertations in esthetics. As we are about to depart, a pilgrim says that he has seen a cross on one of the graves. That is news. Where, exactly, is it? I return to take a look. It is a nondescript carving, discernible with difficulty.

A native young woman upon learning that we are from America looks at us with the gleam of a possible bright future in her eyes. She is wearing a blouse and a skirt that are probably her best clothes. Some mothers in America would be embarrassed to call Good Will to be rid of them. She takes a ring off her middle finger and gives it to us. It's a coiled copper wire one end of which is supposed to be the head of a snake. "So to remember me. I will write you," she says. It is as if we had known these people all our lives. All distinctions vanish. We say good-bye with difficulty.

In Elazig (a southward development of what was Kharpert) where we go from Malatya, the Armenian Liturgy has to be celebrated in the Syrian church. Its priest, Abuna Moushadegh, is more than glad to play host. The Syrian Church is one of the four Lesser Oriental Churches with which we are in communion. Some Armenian monasteries in Cappadocia had within their compounds chapels assigned to Syrian priests and congregations.

Father Moushadegh's church is not much larger than the living room of a spacious American home. There is a stove on the right side of the church whose pipe bends below the ceiling and exits on the opposite side through a hole in the window. The objects that decorate the interior of the church are quaint. They are, I surmise, what the church could afford or was given. One thing that catches the visitor's eye as an interesting antique is the veil (curtain) that hides the altar from view during parts of the Liturgy.

Not all of the Armenian pilgrims came to participate in the Liturgy that day, which was all right. Those of us who were there, along with many of the members of the parish filled the church to capacity. Patriarch Shnork preached the sermon. The Syrian Church is ours, he said, and our church is theirs. Then to the mixed audience he made this declaration: Salvation is possible only through the Christian church. It is the only gate to heaven. There is no other. Deacon Shahan gave a simultaneous translation into Turkish, as usual.

June 13, 1989. Aghtamar is our next destination. One of the most stirring experiences for any Armenian must be seeing Lake Van, the lake of historic Vasbouragan. The first glimpse of its main island from the bus elicits agitated cries. "*That* must be Aghtamar," someone says. "Yes, that must be it!" others concur. There it is indeed, not too far from another even smaller island, like a ship anchored nearby. The water reflects the clear blue of the sky. The late afternoon sun sprinkles itself in glitters forming a strip of uncertain edges across the lake. I think of Shamiram. Did she dream of Ara as her imperial eyes scanned this handiwork of the gods? Did she walk along these shores reading the stars in the stillness of the night? I think of the aqueduct she is reputed to have built. I know it is still serviceable, somewhere not very far from here.

From prehistoric times, where Ara's legend is placed, to World War I this region has given the Armenian people its political and cultural shape. In 1914 the combined Armenian population of the regions east and west of Lake Van must have been more than 375,000. The caza (a subdivision of a vilayet) of Van alone—with Mahmudi, Arjesh and Aljavaz—was an Armenian archbishopric of 108 parishes with a total of 130 churches. Does anyone live in these regions today who recognizes himself or herself as an Armenian?

We are driving through spectacular country. As the highway follows the natural formation of the terrain, Aghtamar disappears and appears again. Not too far from it is the island of Arder. I do not see the islands of Lim and Gdoots. The austerity of the Armenian monks who lived and prayed on them was reputed to be almost beyond human endurance. They were oblivious to comfort. The traditional Lenten diet would be a feast for them.

I instinctively look to my right, away from the lake, as if to catch a glimpse of Narek, the monastery where Saint Gregory, the greatest master of the Armenian language, wrote his immortal Book of Prayers. Had it been written in a more widely known language, it would have been required reading in the great universities around the world for courses in mysticism, religious psychology or the philosophy of religion. The book can agitate the human psyche at its very depth. The masses, beginning with those who lived here, on this land, found in it the power of healing. We are passing through country where the author of that masterpiece walked about. This sea- and landscape played a part in his inspiration. His was one of the most Armenian of monasteries, his soul one of the most Armenian of souls. The monastery has vanished. Nor is there a trace of his tomb.

Our driver is a professional of consummate skill and grace. He sways from side to side as he takes the Mercedes bus along the sharp curves of the road. The islands that had again disappeared come again into view. A word I have seen in history books pops into my mind: Thosbitis. It is the ancient name, derived from the Armenian, of what is now called Van Gölü.

The view of Aghtamar is now clearer. We are all anxious to see the church itself. "There, toward the middle of the island," someone says, "see it?" Yes. That's the reason why we crossed the ocean and are here.

We have to wait till the next day to go to the island and visit the illustrious tenth century Armenian Church of the Holy Cross. This evening, we watch the setting sun from the lakeshore cafe. We sit around small tables drinking an excellent tea and eating the *otlu peynir* the cafe is famous for. "You won't find this cheese anywhere else. They make their own," a friend says. We take pictures. Then I go and stand by the edge of the lake.

I think of King Gagik who had the church built over a period of six or seven years in the first quarter of the tenth century. That is certainly one of the reasons why he is remembered better than many of the kings and princes of his time. I remember hearing of Gagik for the first time in a history course at my Haigazian (Armenian) school in Aleppo, Syria. I remember my teacher, Yetvart Dasnabedian, a bespectacled, lean, vigorous man and a spellbinding lecturer. I see him with that everlasting cigarette between his thin lips. I remember the tips of the long middle and index fingers of his right hand, yellow with nicotine. He was the man who gave me my enthusiasm for the history of my people. When he spoke of the great men of our past, they came alive. It was as if they were there, inviting us to continue their work, to be worthy of them. *Baron* Dasnabedian, as we called him, made me and every student of his admire King Gagik as indeed he should have. But as the years passed, and I went to the sources on my own, my esteem for Gagik gave way to a more critical appraisal. Historians who tell us about Gagik are ambiguous about his character. They were his contemporaries. They knew him personally. Even when he is the object of (clearly biased) praise, one fact stands out: the central concern that informs his policy or behavior is less his people than himself. Moral decency gives way to ambition.

Not consistently, but whenever it was to his own perceived advantage, Gagik sided with one of the most blood-
thirsty oppressors Armenia has ever known: Yusuf, the *vos-
digan* of Armenia. The *vosdigans* were rulers of sorts and tax
collectors for the ameer. A predator by nature, and an
embodiment of human depravity, Yusuf was an accomplished
master at having Armenians shed the blood of Armenians.
He reveled in usurpations and lechery. Gagik allied himself with this man, he was at his side when the fiend was
marching against a rival Armenian prince. Yusuf sent Gagik
a crown in recognition of his services, and thus Gagik became yet another "king." Those were chaotic times. Even
then, however, Gagik could have used his talents in favor
of a united front against a common enemy.

While focussing on the Church of the Holy Cross on its
island, I push Gagik, its "builder," as well as the bishops and
princes who shared in the glory of its consecration, into the
background of my mind. They already had their reward, I
muse. I do not want my gratitude added to it. But I cannot
brush out of my imagination the memory of Manuel, the
architect and chief engraver. I also think of a little known
clergyman, Kevork Havnouni. It was Kevork who put into
use his considerable skills as a negotiator when Isbouk, Yusuf's successor, was about to invade Vasbouragan. Kevork
averted the disaster. The church was built during the peace
that was secured through that negotiation. Would we have
a church at Aghtamar had Kevork failed? I think of all the
slaves, unskilled workers, artisans, masons, carpenters,
assistant engravers who *really* built this church, nameless men
whose sweat is mixed in the mortar that still holds it up, stone
upon stone. Did they have enough to eat in the evening, after
all the hard labor? Did they have a decent place to rest their
wearied bodies?

I think of the multitude of men, women and children
there as the completed church opened its gate. Their voices
come to me across ten turbulent centuries: "You cannot im-

agine how we suffered from the greed of the mighty and their consequent discord," they say to me. "We were a little better off here at Vasbouragan, to be sure, but how could we rest knowing as we did of slaughters and famines all over Armenia? We heard of men and women who sold a child for a loaf of bread. They ate deadly plants to fill their stomachs. And those who had lost their strength fell victim to the unendurable hunger of others." These voices come to me from the past of my people. My own past. "Even then we graced this land," they say. "Look at this church. We built it a thousand years ago for a thousand years. A thousand years have gone by, and lo, here it is!" Then they ask a question. "Will you do your share, you, pilgrims to this holy site, to keep it standing another . . . ?" "Yes, yes, the spirit is willing!" I hear us cry. "The spirit!" they say. "The spirit!" I am confused by the accent with which they say it. Then I hear the voices no more.

There is the island and there the church. The palace of the king, which was surely quite as magnificent as the church, the houses for his servants, family, bodyguard, entourage, aides and guests, even the residence of the catholicos, the fortifications and quays—they are all gone. The church remains.

The next day we pay 10,000 liras each and board two ferries that take us to the island. Now we are on the island of Aghtamar. This is where they, our forefathers of a thousand years ago and more, actually walked. My visual experiences turn into riches of the spirit. This is the water. Those are the hills. That's the firmament. We are seeing what they saw.

I turn to the reliefs on the walls of the church. I wish I could recall all I have read about them, grasp the meaning of, or read the intention behind every little detail. What I see on the western wall gives me an even deeper awareness of Gagik's exclusive ego. There he is, holding in his hands a prominently carved model of the church, offering it to Jesus Christ. He is on one side of a window, Jesus on the other, to the right of the viewer. The Armenian equivalents of the initials J.C. are carved above the head of Jesus Christ—the implication being that the viewer may not recognize him. There are no initials or name over Gagik's head. It occurs to me that any attempt at identifying the king would have been an intolerable slight. Jesus may, but *he* needs no introduction. You look at him, you know who he is. There are other symbolisms on the wall supposed to indicate the piety of the king. His piety! The pharisaism of it all stretches across the centuries and disturbs me.

High above the head of the king there is the relief of the head of an animal. It has deteriorated, but perhaps not beyond the recognition of an expert. Over the head of Christ there is the head of another animal, also deteriorated, but the ears suggest unmistakably that it is a lion. In his left hand Jesus holds the Book of the Gospel. He is quoted as saying, "I am the Light of the World." This phrase occurs in the Gospel of Saint John, who was also assumed to have written the Book of Revelation, in which he speaks of the Lion of the tribe of Juda. It was thought by early commentators that this Lion is a veiled reference to Christ. I suppose that is the reason why the lion's head is where it is on this western wall. I congratulate myself for making the connection, wondering at the same time if someone else has already made it. At the same time it occurs to me that I may be completely wrong.

Below the window between Gagik and Christ there are two angels, each with one wing folded, the other in a position of flight and, owing to the exigency of the design, awkwardly pointing respectively to the king and to the Savior. The angels have auras. They hold a disc bearing the carving of a cross in the traditional Armenian style. Surmounting the whole composition, over the wide decorative band that produces the impression of being to the window what an eyebrow is to an eye, there is, embedded in the wall, a *khachkar* or cross-stone. I am reminded that this is the Church of *Sourp Khach*.

With his magnificent vestments (all the designs of which are meticulously carved), his cope joined by a buckle, his curly hair, his bejewelled crown and, above all, the nimbus around his youthful, handsome face, Gagik, the son of Tere-nig, overpowers the Son of God to whom he is making the gift of a church to be proud of. The nimbus (characteristic of the images of Byzantine emperors) sets his Sacred Majesty apart from ordinary folk. In contrast, the clothes of Jesus are plain. He is smaller in size. It occurs to me that the carver may have thought that Jesus *was* smaller than the king. Some commentators on Luke 19:3 have conjectured that Zaccheus could not see Jesus in the crowd because he, Jesus, was short. I try to be charitable to the carver and assume, against my better judgment, that that is why he gave the king a larger physical stature. The aura around the head of Christ encases irradiations reminiscent of the shape of a cross. His right hand is imparting a blessing to "the western side of the world" which was known to us in medieval times as the side of "the kingdom of the Christians."

We enter the church.

I walk more than once in and out of every room or recess. I look into every nook and cranny as if to uncover some secret that the past persists in keeping from me. The frescoes on the walls of the church proper appear in some instances to have been mutilated on purpose. They are at any rate difficult to see and recognize in the relative dark. I hope my camera will catch some of the details of some of them. The deacons, choir members and others among the pilgrims face the altar and begin to sing selections from the Armenian Divine Liturgy. Our accent has changed no doubt, but the words we are using are identical to the ones that have resonated under these vaults for centuries. They are being sung just now with an extra measure of yearning, or devotion. It is as if those who sang them here since the remote past have come to join us. They make the songs more sincere. They add to their amplitude. It is a short service.

Our Turkish guide tells this Armenian audience that Moslem master builders have learned from this church certain techniques and used them to build mosques. He draws our attention to certain notable features of the architecture. As he speaks to us with informed sympathy I think of the rather unusual word *yergnahart* (skyscraping) that an Armenian historian who was probably there when the church was built uses to describe this very dome. The church was no doubt the tallest building in the area, then.

A bell tower was added in the eighteenth century. A staircase that His Majesty used to walk up to his private room in the church, for comfort and perhaps security, is no longer there. I am inclined to think it regrettable that the original design of the architecture was marred by the addition of the bell tower. But then, I say to myself, the church was not a museum piece until comparatively recent times, and that is something to marvel at and be grateful for. People felt free to modify it to suit the needs of the day. It was still the Church of the Holy Cross where the faithful, not tourists, went, not to look at the carvings and architecture, but to worship the God of their fathers. I see among other tourists a young blond man with a German book in his hand, looking first at the text and then at the reliefs and friezes. He scrutinizes them with characteristic thoroughness, almost inch by inch. Then he explains things to older companions (his parents?) who appear to be less patient.

The government of Turkey has finally come to realize that antiquities can make a lot of money for them. But not all the antiquities are looked after with equal care as evidenced by the condition of the Church of the Holy Cross. There are some "souvenir shops" next to it. No one wanders into them. They are low structures, painted an ugly pistachio green. Their meager wares have nothing to do with the church. One item is a small backgammon set. We buy postcards at the lakeshore cafe on our return. We leave the area with eyes fixed on the church until it vanishes from sight.

Phrases like "open museum" or "laden with history" describe the land of Turkey as well as, if not more aptly than any other land on the face of the earth. At one point in the course of our tour our guide took us to yet another site of interest. As we set foot on the premises someone showed up to collect entrance fees. What we were taken to see turned out at first to be heads or torsos or arms of unidentified statues, lying scattered on the ground over a wide area, some on patches of grass. Is this what we paid our money to see? No, there is the main attraction.

We come to a rather large hole in the ground, with a flat bottom. Our guide talks to the watchman in a tone of embarrassment and guarded anger. "But this is a disgrace," he tells him. The man leaves, comes back with a pail of water, descends into the hole and briskly washes the floor, wiping away the resulting mud. An exquisite mosaic, remarkably well preserved, is revealed. It displays fish at play. This was, our guide says, the floor of a Roman bath.

Our pilgrimage was primarily to Aghtamar. As we head back to Istanbul I reflect on pilgrimages in general, and on this one in particular. The practice of going on pilgrimages is rooted in the ancient belief that gods have their dwelling places on earth, and that they must be visited where they live. In Christianity pilgrimages were born out of the desire to walk where the Incarnate Lord did. Then they were made to the tombs of the martyrs, for it was thought that divine power attached to the bodies of these saints, notably to their bones. Churches were pilgrimage destinations when they were shrines of relics. People went to these churches to avail themselves of the power that was there, to beseech God to grant such blessings as health and fertility. They also went there to pray to the martyr-saint to intercede with God for their salvation. Did any of us come to the Church of the Holy Cross for any of these reasons? How was our trip a *pilgrimage*? Each "pilgrim" would have to answer this question for himself or herself. Yet I venture to say that our common motive was, in addition to entertainment, a desire to remember; to "remember" what some of us did not know in the first place. It was a return to our roots. What made it a pilgrimage was that the roots we were returning to were religious. Or at least Patriarch Shnork perceived it to be that.

Whether a Christian should go on pilgrimages has been a matter of dispute among various divines. There have been opinions against it beginning with those of Saint John, the fourth evangelist (". . . the hour cometh, when ye shall neither in this mountain nor yet at Jerusalem, worship the Father.") Several Fathers of the church have written against excesses or wrong motivations that cause a pilgrimage to do more evil than good.

Many members of our pilgrimage are, to be sure, deeply pious. That piety has a long tradition behind it. Istanbul is, after all, the only place, after Armenia and Jerusalem, where the Armenian Church has had a continuous existence for centuries. But tradition will sometimes encourage the letter against the spirit, and piety can easily be limited to external practices. Or it can turn into superstition. Standing in front of the church at Aghtamar, a pilgrim pulls out of his wallet a carefully folded piece of paper. This is a very old document, he says, and lets me look at it. It is obvious from the condition of the paper and from the calligraphy of the text that it is only a few decades old. The text lists a number of diseases and misfortunes. So long as I have this in my pocket I am safe, the man says.

As I think of these matters on the bus on the way back from the focal point of our pilgrimage some telling scenes revisit my mind. *Item*: In one of the cities we visit, a member of the choir is seen standing at the door of the church, leaning against the jamb, one foot in the church, the other out. He is smoking a cigarette, absentmindedly blowing every other puff of smoke into the church. He is at the same time crossing himself dutifully, even bowing slightly as the rite requires. *Item*: One member of the pilgrimage is a bit tipsy at least some of the time. Once or twice he is not there when the bus is full and ready to go. He seldom actually attends a service, but whenever we enter a completely empty, partially ruined church he makes a point of finding the altar, crosses himself and is impeccably reverent. *Item*: The Divine Liturgy is being celebrated. A pilgrim is singing in the choir with a camera hanging around his neck, over his *shabig* (robe). He moves about, positions himself for good shots while singing, clicks the camera, flash flashing, whenever the Patriarch or anyone of any visual appeal makes a move.

I realize that for all anyone knows no such solemn services may be held in these Armenian churches again, and it is important that a record be kept. At the same time I cannot avoid the feeling that the acts of worship we are engaging in during this pilgrimage are in the minds of a sizable minority at least not much more than photo opportunities.

We are traveling westward. Diyarbakir is on the way. This is the city, on the right bank of the Tigris, that the Romans called Amida. It was taken by the Sassanians and retaken a number of times. We call it Dikranakerd with some justification; the town's Ulu Jami (Great Mosque) stands where the old Sassanian palace used to be, which was in turn built over a royal residence of our Tigran the Great.

In 1895 the vilayet of Diyarbakir was identified as one of the six most densely populated by Armenians within the Ottoman Empire. The purpose of the massacres that were perpetrated in that year was to thin this population out to the point where they would no longer be a noticeable "minority," and remove any justification for intervention by European and other powers for the purpose of having the human rights of a minority respected. I asked someone the number of Armenians living in Diyarbakir today. He answered with a question: "Twenty-five?"

Diyarbakir is a colorful city. It is colorful with the succulent fruits in the markets, the ankle-length ample dresses worn by the women, the distinctive headgear of Kurdish men, horse-drawn contraptions on wheels alongside automobiles and trucks, that carry both merchandise and people. As I watch a very busy plaza I remember hearing as a child about Diyarbakir's big watermelons and scorpions. Watermelons are sold in abundance. They are no larger than watermelons in any American city, but I am told they are singularly sweet. I do not see any scorpions—not in the streets. A woman, obviously deranged, spits at us and tries to hit one of the women in our group, angry that we are non-Moslem foreigners. A man is selling cold tamarind ade out of a metal vessel tied to his back. He bends down ceremoniously to fill a brass cup for a customer. He uses the same three cups for all of his customers.

There is a chapel within the enclave of the Church of Saint Kirakos where the Divine Liturgy was celebrated on that day for the natives and for us. Patriarch Shnork preached the sermon. It was the feast of Saints Sahak and Mesrob. The Patriarch told us who they were, what they did, and that we should be faithful to their work, preserve the spiritual and cultural riches they bequeathed to us. It pains me to assume that a year from now the feast of the Translators will come and go, and any Armenians still living in this city will not know the difference.

After the services in the chapel, we visit the Church of Saint Kirakos. It is a spacious, impressive structure. Someone sees me counting the altars. There are seven of them, he says. Discounting the altars for a moment, I get the vague impression that the architect must have been influenced by the interior design of mosques. The church is in a sorry state of deterioration. A good portion of the light streams in through gaping holes that time and neglect have opened in the ceiling. We hear rumors to the effect that the Patriarch is paying an official visit to the provincial governor. Will he ask for permission to restore the church? For whom?

We visit Sis, the present-day Kozan, toward the end of our journey. The buses bring us to a plaza in the city, at a relatively high altitude. From here cabs will take us closer to the Castle of Levon, he being arguably the most illustrious of the Armenian kings of Cilicia. The last stretch of the way to the Castle is not accessible to wheeled vehicles. Some of the pilgrims take a look at the ruins of it atop the hill and discover that they are not all that anxious to see its interior after all. Those of us who feel rugged enough to undertake the ascent are rewarded with a memorable panoramic view, flat lands extending beyond the town at the foot of the hill. The town has sprawled since medieval times, but it has not become a big city. This was where the Armenian Catholicos of Cilicia resided before World War I; the city where my father was ordained a priest.

The last Catholicos of Cilicia consecrated in Sis (in 1903, at age 54) was Sahag Khabayan. His coadjutor, Papken Guleserian, consecrated in Aleppo in 1934, was thus the first catholicos of "the Great House of Cilicia," whose title squared with the facts only partially. He was the catholicos of the *people* of Cilicia. When the Armenians left that land in the early 1920's, Catholicos Sahag was among them—left with not much more than his title and some standing among his people. He was an old man when my father took me to see him in Aleppo, at the residence of someone who, judging from my remembered impression of the house, must have been quite wealthy. I was a little boy. "We are going to see an important man. You will remember his name when you grow up. You will be proud of having seen him personally. Don't forget; you call him 'Vehapar Der.' You kiss his holy hand and he will put it on your head and bless you," my father said. My memory of Catholicos Sahag's face is so vivid that I could paint it on a canvas if I had the talent. I was sitting on one side of a mahogany desk. He was behind it talking to my father. Unexpectedly and to my utter shock the Catholicos pulled open a drawer, took out a bottle, poured himself a jigger of *raki* and drank it. My father looked at me and realized what was going on in my little head. Later in the street he said, "He takes it as medicine." I knew what my father was trying to do. I am in Sis; Catholicos Sahag should not have been driven from this place.

As I enter through what seems to be the main gate of the castle I see inscriptions in Arabic on either side of the gate which I try in vain to unscramble. I am frustrated. If only I could read a name! Inside the castle in the various chambers people I think must have lived there come back before my eyes to a gossamer life. I try without much success to reconstruct their intrigues, their moments of splendor, their loves and pains. I had seen at one point during the ascent that the castle was quite extensive. Is this where Levon, the "King of All Armenians," brought his second wife, Sibyl, a girl in her early teens, when he himself was sixty? Was he sitting here when he ordered that his cousin's eyes be gouged out? I imagine King Hetoum hopping around from room to room. I look out of an opening and think of the battles that were fought in defense of this fortification, of this piece of land. Then I remember that fateful year, 1375, one of the six or seven most important dates of our history. After yet another battle King and Catholicos surrender and the Armenian kingdom comes to an end, never again to be revived.

We are eventually on our way to Derik, a village situated about 25 miles west of Mardin, a predominantly Kurdish town. On the way up to the Armenian Church of Saint Kevork the women of our group are advised not to walk arm in arm with their husbands. Somebody says that the Prime Minister of Turkey was once seen on television with his arm around his wife and almost lost his job. No one takes the advice seriously. Children, not too clean but quite well nourished, and a number of idle adults look at us curiously, without apparent malice. Here too the few Armenians who have remained have lost their language, but not their faith. Nor have they lost a most characteristic Armenian trait: hospitality. These people are not rich, but that does not prevent them from being generous. Armenians? From Istanbul? America? From where? France? Uruguay? Arms open, and the embrace is warm. We respond. It is the embrace of people who have *missed* each other.

The adult women, notably those over 35, wear flower-patterned, ample, ankle-length dresses we have seen in Diyarbakir. Their faces are framed with a white kerchief that also covers their shoulders. Over the kerchief on the head they wear a knit, often red and black cap hiding part of the forehead. Thus only the face and the hands are uncovered. At Derik we, all 70 of us, are served boiled lamb, pilaf, *tahn* (water-diluted yogurt), shepherd's salad and fruit.

A woman at one corner of the courtyard is doing the pots and pans and plates. Piles of them. She washes them on the floor, in a crouched position. She is fully dressed, shawl, cap and all. As she sees me with a camera walking toward her she springs to her feet. I cannot help but notice the effortless agility with which she does so. I ask her to please continue working. She crouches back, holds up a dish and a sudsy cloth and looks at the camera most seriously. I wait a second. Will she smile? Her expression does not change.

There were once five Armenian churches here. A native tells me that the current Armenian population of the city is between 100 and 150. The original edifice of the church is some 300 years old. The interior of the church is decorated with, here and there, religious pictures in nearly shadeless, vivid colors painted on rectangular pieces of a velvet-like material. My interlocutor tells me that in order to prevent the requisition of the building by the state a prominent individual, Garabed Kechejioglu, acquired it as a home for himself, and lets it be used as a house of worship.

\* \* \*

The warmest hospitality is again shown us at Vakiflikoy which we visit after Derik. Vakif or Vakiflikoy is a suburb of Samandag, the former Seleucia Pieria, the port of Antioch where large numbers of Armenians had lived at least since the time of Tigran the Great. "You've heard of Musadag. That's Musadag over there," someone says to me pointing to a prominent hill in the distance.

Vakiflikoy is now a village with a meager but almost entirely Armenian population. To get there we drive through another village that is almost entirely Greek. In the course of driving through this village I discover within myself, I must confess, a feeling that I do not like and do not want to have. When someone says to me, "There are almost no Turks in this village," I secretly, very much in spite of myself, feel a little more at ease. It's an absurd feeling in this place at this time. I refuse to recognize it, but there it is.

As we enter the church compound I observe that on a slightly elevated section of the courtyard by the wall there are four cauldrons. Three are covered with deep pans placed on them upside down. Wood is burning under the cauldrons. A fifth, shallower pot is full of simmering butter or animal fat—I do not know which—with what look like chunks of suet floating in it. We shall be eating *harissa*—the real thing!—after the *badarak*.

As was his habit the Patriarch preached about the saints of the day, seizing the opportunity to teach a bit of Armenian history, with the appropriate moral. He evoked the memories of King Drtad, his queen Ashkhen, and his sister Khosrovitoukhd.

After the service all available tables are hurriedly occupied by some of the guests in the courtyard. Others mill about in search of a convenient place for themselves. A man ladles out the meat and wheat mixture beaten to the consistency of pulp, tops it with spoonfuls of hot fat, then gives the plates to young men and women who serve the guests.

The Patriarch sat at a table along one side of the court-

yard. Next to him was the world's oldest Armenian clergyman, Der Ghevont Kartounian, in his nineties and not yet
retired. The Patriarch was of course served first. He was
not happy with the melted glistening substance covering his
*harissa*. He asked for another serving without it. Some of
us are encouraged by his example and do likewise. "But
that's where all the taste is!" someone says. I find myself
regretting my concern about cholesterol. These people have
worked so very hard. They are doing their best to please
their guests, guests who will not reciprocate, many, perhaps
all of whom they will never see again.

A thin, tall, rather elderly man with white crew cut hair,
wearing an old suit a size too large, keeps stirring the *harissa*
while his friend continues to ladle it out. I observe that very
few men are doing any of the work. I recall something seen
once in a while along the highways of the interior of Turkey:
A man rides his donkey. Behind him walks his woman,
sometimes carrying a basket.

The Church of Saint Mary at Vakiflikoy has a bell tower.
It consists of four upright iron bars, supporting a narrower
set of about equal length, bent at the top and coming to a
point from which hangs a little bell. It stands at one corner
of the courtyard.

Even less glamorous is the Church of Saint Gregory the
Enlightener at Kirikhan. When I was a child Kirikhan was
part of Syria, which was in turn under French mandate. It
was a thriving little community of Armenians. Kirikhan is now
a village in Turkey. The interior of the church is entirely bare
except for a picture below which there is an oblong sand-
box for burning votary candles. Kirikhan is not far from Iskenderun, formerly known as Alexandretta. It was founded
to celebrate the victory of Alexander (Iskender) the Great
against the Persians in 333 BC. Only about 50 years ago Iskenderun was a Syrian port city in the province of then Sanjak, now Hatay. In the cafes one still hears Arabic. There are

restaurants on the boulevard along the Mediterranean Sea where fish is expensive but, if you know how to choose and do not mind the price, superb.

Armenian life has understandably dwindled here too since the transfer of the territory to Turkey. The nineteenth-century Church of the Forty Martyrs (*Karasoun Mangants*) appears nevertheless to be holding steady. It is under the care of Father Serovpe Gulian, who had been assisted until before our visit by Messrs. Tabash, Demirel, Kisadour, Dolash and Silahli.

Not all the Armenian church buildings in Anatolu have crumbled and disappeared or are about to. There is, for example, the former Armenian Church of the Holy Mother of God (Sourp Asdwadzadzin) of Gaziantep. This town is the former Aintab, near historic Rhomcla, where Saint Nersess the Graceful lived, wrote, governed the church, sought the unification of the entire Christian church, and reconciled warring Armenian princes to each other in the twelfth century. There is no Armenian living in Aintab today.

The Armenian masses of that city spoke Turkish for the last 200 years or more, but a careful study of the vocabulary used by both the Armenians and the Turks of the region has convinced some scholars that Armenian was the dominant language there. This was the case in all probability until Janissaries began to cut the tongues of those who did not speak Turkish. (The Janissaries constituted for a long time the standing army of the Ottoman Empire. The corps began with 1,000 Christian youths recruited in 1330. Their army of about 150,000 soldiers became so unruly by the beginning of the nineteenth century that they were shot, burned and hanged out of existence in 1826.) Also indicative of the once Armenian Christian culture of the region of Aintab is the amazing circumstance that until the beginning of this century there were grandmothers in some entirely Moslem households, who would insist on having their own (Armenian) priests minister to their religious needs.

Aintab is one of the cities famous for the self-defense of

its Armenian population against the Turks. This was in 1920. Upon the occupation of Aintab by the British, then by the French at the conclusion of World War I, 17,000 of the Armenians who had been deported in 1915 returned to their homes (18,000 had perished). When the French wavered in their determination to fight the Turks and hold on to their mandate, the Armenians resolved to defend themselves. They could not trust the Turkish promises that they would not be harmed. The memory of 1915 was still too fresh, and they had heard of the massacres of Marash only 50 miles northeast of them.

The vacillations of the French did not come altogether as a surprise. The Armenians had secretly gathered piles of stones in their homes. They had built passages connecting nearly all the houses. The entire Armenian quarter had become a maze through which the inhabitants could communicate with each other. All able-bodied males between the ages of seven and 70 were mobilized. Women were given assignments of their own. When, on April 1, the Turks attacked, men, women and children carried the stones out, and within hours barricades were erected under the supervision of masons strategically stationed. Their section of the city, surrounded by Turks on three sides, became a nearly impregnable stronghold.

For all intents and purposes the Armenian quarter of Aintab was almost overnight a mini-state with all the departments that a state needs in time of war. There were committees in charge of the equitable distribution of available food; of negotiations with the enemy, and with the French; of strategy and tactics; of conscription; of the manufacture of weapons; and of intelligence. Centers were created to treat the wounded. Military police and tribunals were set up to punish any who might venture to fish in troubled waters. Craftsmen and smiths shaped every pipe they could lay their hands on into primitive weapons. They made bombs. They even made a cannon, the much celebrated *Vrezh* (revenge). They mounted it on the front wheels of a buggy and made a point—with necessary precautions taken not to show too much—of putting it on a rooftop for the enemy to see. The cannon had to be weighted down with big stones and tied with heavy chains, for it had the nasty tendency of turning around each time it was fired. It could be aimed in the general direction of the enemy, though only the Lord knew where the iron shreds it spewed out would land. But it did the trick. When the Turks heard its boom, they could only think that their very existence was being threatened.

The Armenians were poorly armed. Other than the primitive bombs they had made, all they had were a few hundred Mausers, double-barreled hunting guns and revolvers. They were always short of ammunition. As I write this, I recall the woman I met in her later years. She must have been baptized as Manoushag, though everyone knew her as Imanem Mennoush. She had an astonishing memory and must have had, in her prime, nerves of steel. She would brave the enemy fire at night and, in case of extreme urgency, in broad daylight, go to the French garrison—where French soldiers did not do much more than watch the show—and come back with sackfuls of bullets.

My father, a priest, was president of the National Council, directing the entire operation. He did not have a desk. He had a simple escritoire where the buck stopped. When no volunteer was found for dangerous missions, he undertook them. By the end of May, after many ups and downs and about 100 casualties, the Armenians had won the battle. But then the French finally withdrew from the region, unable or unwilling to resist the advancing Turkish Kemalist troops. The Armenians once again left their homes, vineyards, businesses, and in carts, on animals or on foot, took the road to Aleppo and beyond.

Because of the number of its schools (they were opening an Armenian lyceum as late as 1913!) and its generally very active rich collective cultural life, Aintab was known as the

Athens of Anatolia. After the stubborn resistance the French called it the Armenian Verdun, the French city on the Meuse where in 1916 Petain decisively defeated a German offensive.

My father survived the war with the Turks. He was shot dead in 1934 by an Armenian, in our home in Aleppo. He had decided to live in this Syrian city with his people to whom the Arabs had given refuge. The murderer had his grudges, but there were rumors to the effect that individuals who had an Armenian political axe to grind had egged him on. It is in those trying circumstances that, as a young boy, I got to know Mennoush well. She handed me a piece of paper one day. "I, I should have died, not your father, not he," she lamented. "If it were possible to give my life to bring him back, I would do it a thousand times." On the piece of paper was a poem about my father's deeds. In Turkish, with Armenian characters. "Keep it. I hope you will read it when you are as old as I am," she said. She had a talent for composing verses, but she had to dictate them to someone. She herself could neither write nor read.

Patriarch Shnork was kind enough to have us accompany him in his minibus on his way to Hatay. We were going to see what had been the Armenian church of Aintab. This was an unscheduled trip. The Patriarch had heard about the church and wanted to see it. The fact that it was my father's church was an added incentive for us.

As we boarded the minibus I became aware, now more clearly, that the group has been traveling on the open roads under the protective attention of troopers. They were there because the Patriarch had, before departure, advised the proper authorities that he would make this tour. Between cities the police of one locality would pass on to the next the responsibility of keeping an eye on the minibus. The minibus was outfitted with a couch for the Patriarch to rest on when he felt tired. During this part of the trip the Patriarch told me of his many relatives, and of the two children—now

young men—whom he had adopted to save them from in-
digence and ignorance. "The law allows it," he said, as if
thankful that the law let him give expression to his charitable
instincts.

The pilgrims were not scheduled to visit Gaziantep. After
1920 the Armenian church there had been turned into a jail.
The information we had was that it had been remodeled and
converted into a mosque. A large number of the mosques in
Turkey, some of the most majestic among them, were Christian houses of worship.

A four-lane highway led us into the town. Our problem
then was to find the church in the old city. As we got there
we did not ask, Where is the old Armenian church? Rather,
we enquired about "the mosque which used to be a jail."

The Armenian church of Gaziantep is an imposing building, 31 meters high, about one-third of the height taken up
by the drum and the Byzantine-style dome that caps it. The
corners of the edifice as well as its cornices and arched windows are built with alternating rows of black granite and white
*esembek* stone. "The walls are thick enough," my father, Der
Nersess Avak Kahana Tavoukdjian, who for years celebrated
the Divine Liturgy in that church, used to tell me, "for a
buggy to be drawn on them by a horse." The original plan
was the work of Sarkis Bey Balian, architect to the sultan,
of Palace of Dolma Bahche Fame. But that plan was found
too modest by the local architect, Sarkis Ousta Kadehjian,
who modified and enlarged it by one third. It took 17 years
to construct the ensuing complex structure, and by the time
the cross was mounted on the dome on October 18, 1893,
the church had cost 10,000 Ottoman gold liras, in addition
to the donated labor of Armenian skilled workers. Master
builder Kadehjian, by the way, had never gone to school.

The conversion of the church to mosque was not quite
completed when we saw it in June. A window in the shape
of a cross in the pediment of the facade had been modified,
and all Christian symbols removed or obliterated. The bell

tower was made into a minaret, with the addition of a second one, symmetrically placed. A woman who saw us look at and photograph the building invited us to see the interior with its red and white marble embellishments, but the door was locked. She kept knocking. No one answered.

The last Armenians left Aintab in 1922. Some had returned after 1920 in the hope of reclaiming the properties they had left behind. What they found out was that justice was not the concern of the new "owners." In some instances the usurpers were rid of the claims by simply poisoning the claimants.

I leave my father's church, the new mosque, struck by the irony of the situation. The Turks had pulled down all the crosses, but they could not very well reshape the mighty building, itself built in the shape of the Cross. They would have to worship Allah, or Tanri, as they now call Him as part of an effort to purify the Turkish language, in a cruciform building after all. The past has a way of not permitting itself to be eradicated.

It is certainly no exaggeration to say that Asia Minor is an enviable piece of real estate, which is at least partly why every tribe and combination of tribes that came to know of, or stumbled upon, it sought to be its master. And that of course makes it even more valuable. As already noted, almost every mile of Turkey is evocative of a piece of history. In many instances habitats have remained intact for hundreds of years. The caves and underground chambers in historic Cappadocia are a case in point. The monks who lived there included Armenians, Saint Aristakess (†333), the son of Gregory the Enlightener, among them.

Much of the landscape from one end of Turkey to the other is dazzling. The land is fertile. Visitors in late spring and early summer are bound to be impressed by the abundance of fruits, vegetables, bread, dairy products, meats, poultry and fish—all of which are available at, in American terms, reasonable prices, and this in a country where agribusiness is only beginning.

Sheep seem to be everywhere in the country, led around sometimes by young boys, poor but healthy looking. Patriarch Shnork himself was one such boy at Igdeli, a village situated roughly half way between Yozgat and Kayseri. At about eight years of age he entered the service of a Turkish farmer to tend his sheep, rams and oxen. Life was not easy. On a particularly trying day he spontaneously cried, "My God, when wilt thou deliver me from this torment?" That was his first prayer, as he recalled, and it was answered. He was moved to the orphanage in Lebanon. He was thus separated from his mother, whom he saw again, as a bishop, in Istanbul after a separation of 33 years.

The uprooted boy Arshag, destined to become Archbishop Shnork, Patriarch of the Armenians of Turkey, was about ten years old when he saw Armenian letters, and witnessed a celebration of the Armenian liturgy for the very first time. Upon hearing the name Jesus, again for the first time at around ten, he asked, "Who is Jesus? Was he Armenian?" Eventually Arshag went to study at the Armenian Seminary of Jerusalem, and was ordained in 1935. In time he became the principal of various schools, including the Seminary of Antelias, priest of the Armenians of London, parish priest in New Jersey, Primate of the Armenian Diocese of California and, before his election as Patriarch, Chief Sacristan of the Armenian Monastery of Jerusalem. He has translated devotional works from the English, and has authored some fifteen books and monographs. The word "saintly" is the most frequently associated with his name by those who knew him. The vice he abhorred most, he said to me, is that of the Prodigal Son: wasteful, riotous living. This was one reason why he was profoundly displeased with the conduct of the Armenian Patriarch, Yeghishe Derderian of Jerusalem. He wrote a volume documenting the latter's lawlessness, and forbade the mention of his name during the

Divine Liturgy in the churches under his jurisdiction.

Only once have I myself detected anything approaching anger in Archbishop Shnork's tone of voice. He was pointing out that the Turkish government would not recognize Armenian organizations as legal entities, that it was difficult if not impossible to get permits for renovating, let alone building churches, and that there were artificial obstacles in the way of running the Armenian schools as they should be run.

Elected in 1961 as the eighty-second Patriarch of the Armenians of Turkey, Archbishop Shnork was called upon principally to guide his flock, improve its status as a religious community, see to it that the churches remain open and alive, bring his share in the governance of the Armenian Church generally, and maintain ecumenical relations. There were crises in all of these areas, but the main area where Archbishop Shnork's mettle as a diplomat was always being tested was that of his formal relations with the Turkish government, particularly after Mr. Yanikian's killing of two Turkish diplomats in Los Angeles in 1971. Every time a Turkish official was assassinated by ASALA, for example, the Patriarch sent expressions of regret to Turkish authorities. In 1982 he initiated a drive to raise money for the families of the victims of the attack at Ankara. A year later the Armenians of Turkey organized a demonstration at Taksim plaza in Istanbul against the assassinations by Armenians of Turkish diplomats abroad. At about the same period explosives were thrown more than once by unknown individuals seeking to damage the Mother Church of *Sourp Asdwadzadzin* as well as the Patriarchate. One such attack occurred on the morning of January 6, 1978. In July of the same year, had not an attempt at arson been detected in time by the staff, the entire Patriarchate would have gone up in flames. Throughout this period of tension Patriarch Shnork condemned "all terrorism," and received assurances from President Evren, for example, on February 12, 1982, that "it never occurs to us to avenge ourselves in response to these crimes [of terrorism abroad] on our Armenian compatriots."

It is not to be imagined that all the Armenians of Turkey live in constant tension. They are born here. They are adjusted. This is their country, they like it, and many would not dream of uprooting themselves and living elsewhere. They do enjoy the freedom they have in areas of social togetherness and worship. At the same time the aim of the government's policy remains clear. It does not want to create within the Turkish nation another national entity with a "center" of its own. This is why the government will not look kindly on the Patriarchate's becoming a legal entity. "The patriarchate" is "the patriarch" in practically every aspect of its operations, including the financial. The government will not allow the Armenians to form an assembly of their own, with delegates from various locations, to work toward the preservation of their identity and the enrichment of their church and culture. It will go by the antiquated principle of Armenian "neighborhoods" at a time when the demography of Istanbul has changed and there are no such neighborhoods to speak of.

Why are all these monkey wrenches thrown into the wheels of the Armenian religious/cultural organizations in Turkey? Because, one may speculate, a more liberal course of action would impart to the members of the Armenian minority a collective consciousness of their own. The Turks in their effort to prevent this are in effect continuing the basic policy that suggested the Genocide—the elimination of the Armenian presence in Turkey, except that a policy of subtle repression will do it in gentler ways. It will do it over a long period of time. But the Genocide was not only immoral. It was idiotic. What have the Turks gained from it? Nothing, of course. What did they lose? Plenty. Assuming for a moment, for the sake of argument, that the Armenians would indeed have sided with Turkey's enemy during World War I, there were certainly much more humane ways of preventing that eventuality. The Turks have always had an image problem. One of the definitions that the dictionary gives of "Turk" is "one who is cruel, hardhearted, or tyrannical." The Genocide confirms that definition, which is obviously why the Turks deny it strenuously.

Perhaps the reason why Germany does—and Turkey does not—admit to the holocaust each has unleashed is that German culture is informed by Christianity with its emphasis on sin and repentance. Turkey has no Martin Luther. Sin and repentance, as distinct from disobedience and punishment, are notions that Islam pretty much lacks. Turkey appears to be under the impression moreover, political considerations aside, that its moral sensitivity is confirmed by its putative innocence of the Genocide. But the facts being what they are, that is a clear mistake. The morality of a collectivity is confirmed when it admits its malefaction and proclaims its regret.

To an American—a citizen of a pluralistic society—Turkish governmental policy with regard to an ethnic and religious minority should be difficult to comprehend. The Armenians of Turkey, who live across the border from Armenia, are less in contact with it than are American-Armenians whom thousands of miles of land and ocean separate from their historic fatherland. That too is odd.

If one looks at the petitions that the Patriarch was always presenting to the government—and receiving polite assurances that were subsequently ignored—one cannot escape the conclusion that Turkish/Armenian relations are defined by Turkey's forcibly ambivalent attitude toward nationalism. On the one hand, the post-Ottoman nationalism that created today's Turkey cannot be faulted. On the other, the dismemberment (and reduction to a mere peninsula) to which other nationalisms subjected the Ottoman Empire cannot be remembered by the Turks with any degree of pride. National aspirations are always attractive—so long as they are one's own. It is for this reason that nationalist Turkey will not allow minority nationalisms. And what complicates the situation is that Turkey, formally a secular state, knows only too well that religion and nationalism can easily intertwine. So when the authorities forbid any Armenian clergyman to set foot within an Armenian school at any time, a double purpose is served—official secularism is preserved, and the possible infusion, into the heads and hearts of minorities, of non-Turkish nationalistic notions is kept at bay.

Again, however, Turkey will have its reputation to consider. As the Armenian world community becomes stronger in time, and the circumstances of the Genocide become more widely known, it will be difficult to prevent more individuals and collective bodies from openly condemning it, at least in the West. The consequence of that eventuality will be something of an irony in the sense that Turkey's further alienation from the West will be a threat to the realization of Ataturk's fondest dreams.

And thereon depends of course the fate of the Armenians of Turkey. As noted earlier, an as yet small number of Armenian young men and women operate on the assumption that a prudent self-adjustment to the facts of life in their country does not spell their extinction as members of the Armenian Church. With a cautious yet vigorous program of public relations, they feel, it should be possible to put an end to, or at least reduce to a minimum, dispossessions and other deleterious measures, and go on doing the job of the church which is to fill its members with the faith of Gregory the Enlightener. That faith is national in a sense, but it is not nationalistic in that it has universal dimensions.

But that requires more than going through the motions, and reciting precomposed prayers—although such routine performances may be necessary to keep the shell of the church. One must work toward the day when the church will be filled with the Spirit again. Needed are properly educated, committed clergymen. And that too, the younger men and women claim, is possible. To make all this come true one has to *believe* that it is realizable. One must not be defeated in one's optimism. The idea here is not so much to preserve a tradition—although that is very much in the picture—as to chart a way, bound to be steep and narrow, and proceed to scale it.

A symbolic detail comes to mind. There is at Balat, a section of Istanbul, the church of *Charkhapan Sourp Asdwadzadzin* (Evil-preventer Holy Mother of God), a church with a long, complex, engrossing history. Petitions presented to its black Virgin, whose image hangs to the right of the main altar, have been answered with unusual frequency, and the church has become a shrine. While we were inside the church four Moslem Kurdish women stood at the entrance of the church and removed their shoes before proceeding further. "A lot of them come, and they are very respectful," explained the warden. "They remove their shoes as you see, which is something the Armenians never do," she added. I saw some crutches that were left in one corner of the church, and I inquired about the healings. "Three or four *aylazks* [she meant Moslems] are healed every year," she said.

I remembered that earlier the warden had inquired about our identity before unlocking the door to let us in. "Why do you keep the door locked?" I asked. "There are thefts and vandalisms," she said. There was the paradox. Why damage something that can heal?

The situation in Turkey has something to tell us about the Armenian diaspora, perhaps all diasporas. There can be little doubt that had it not been for the Armenian Church there would be no Armenians in Turkey today. The church has created the common Armenian consciousness and sustained it through time, through the multiplicity of countries where Armenians live, and the variety of languages they speak. The implication is that the only viable bond of togetherness is the awareness that Armenian creativity, as perhaps all creativity, is rooted in faith, that its fruits are of universal value, and that the world should be made to partake of these fruits for our and the world's own good.

When Patriarch Shnork began his incumbency there were in Turkey some 80,000 Armenians. Their number now is about half that, or less. This remnant may survive and even prosper if its leaders dedicate themselves to ideals that transcend mere survival, and if Turkey itself comes to realize that the total freedom of religious and cultural self-expression and the right to the means of achieving these (churches, schools, halls, assemblies, minority national elections, ownership of real estate by legal entities, etc.) must be extended to everyone and to every minority for the good of the country itself. A familiar melody is pleasant to listen to, but a choir of many voices is richer. It is also more rewarding. Turkey would like to be accepted as a member of the European Community. That would be a good thing for everyone concerned, for then the Turkish government might come to realize that *noblesse oblige*. At any rate, one way of getting to be a member of that Community is to deserve such membership. This means that Turkey should extend to all its citizens all rights and freedoms that citizens of the European Community take for granted.